D0209837

Finder

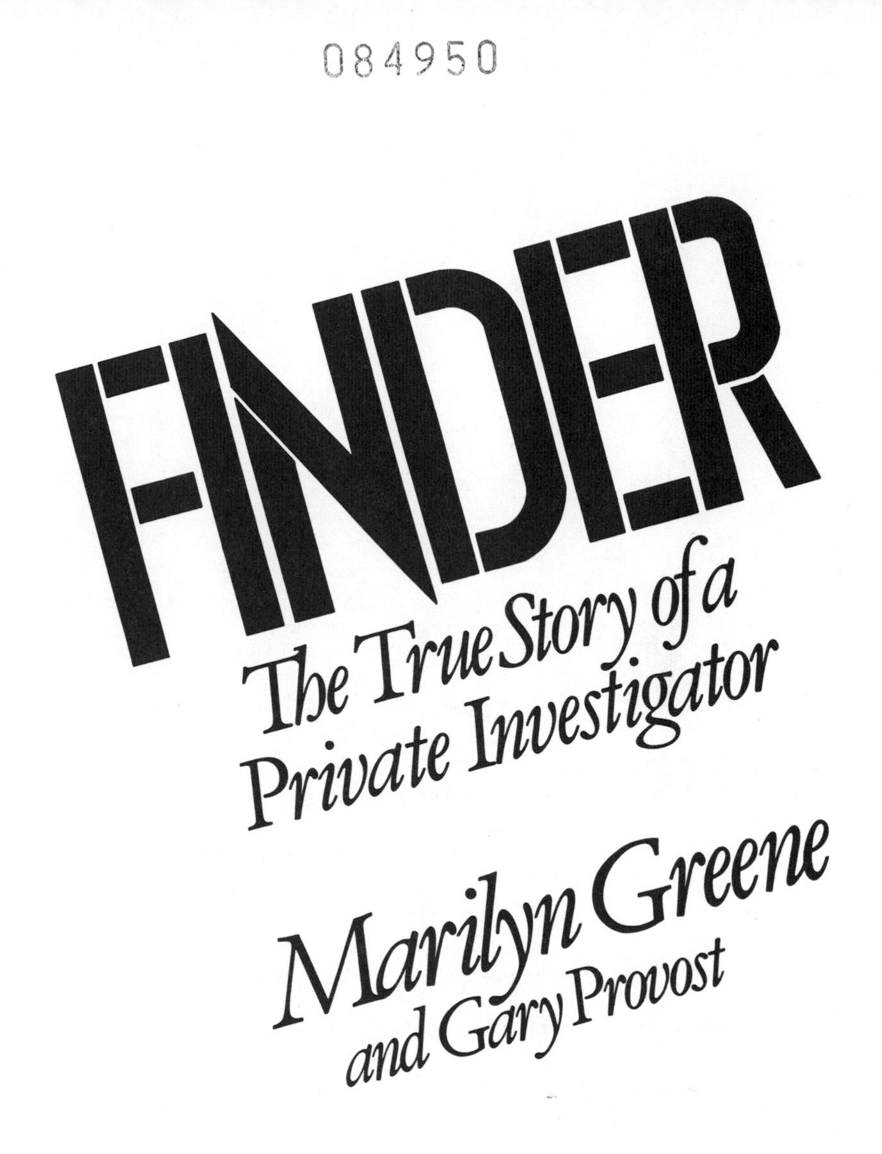

Crown Publishers, Inc., New York

Published by Crown Publishers, Inc., 225 Park Avenue South, New York, New York 10003 and represented in Canada by the Canadian MANDA Group

CROWN is a trademark of Crown Publishers, Inc.

Manufactured in the United States of America

Library of Congress Cataloging-in-Publication Data

Greene, Marilyn.
Finder.

1. Greene, Marilyn. 2. Women detectives—United States—Biography. 3. Missing persons—United States—Investigation. I. Provost, Gary, 1944– . II. Title.
HV8083.G74A3 1987 363.2′89′0924 [B] 87-15449
ISBN 0-517-56490-4

10 9 8 7 6 5 4 3 2 1

First Edition

For Gail, the greatest find of my life.
G. P.

Authors' Note

We have tried to write a book that is honest as well as one that is sensitive to the confidentiality of client relationships. In most cases we have changed the names of clients and their families and, in many cases, minor details which might identify them. But everything else is true. The people in this book are real. The events we relate actually occurred.

M. G. and G. P.

Prologue

I search for missing people. I suppose that sounds glamorous to a fan of television detective shows, where a person who disappears usually takes with him a sack of money, a beautiful lover, or an explosive secret. But in real life, people disappear for reasons more complex and more tragic, and the job of finding them does not require smoking pistols or flashy cars.

I enjoy an exciting TV drama as much as the next person, but in real life, private-investigative work is not like "Magnum P.I." It can't be. The stakes are too high. There is no time for self-congratulation. Once I went on an out-of-state trip to work on five different cases. Things went well and I found four of the people I was looking for. When I came back I told a friend. She was impressed.

"Gee," she said, "four out of five. That's great news."

"Not for the mother of the fifth child," I said.

I look for people who are lost in the wilderness, or who are voluntarily missing, who are homicide victims or children who have been abducted by a stranger or by a parent. I have found hundreds of missing adults and children in twenty-five states, and I love what I do, but it is not glamorous.

When I was asked to tell my story, I saw it as a chance to talk about the missing-person problem as it really is. My hope is that by sharing my story I can also share my concern, and perhaps raise awareness of the missing-person problem in America, so that someday there won't have to be a fifth child who never comes home.

Finder

1

When I was eighteen I lived in Albany, New York, and I had two dreams.

One dream was to become a state trooper. So, shortly after I got out of high school, I made an appointment to pick up an application at the state-police barracks. I phoned ahead, and when I got there I was greeted by a tall, good-looking trooper.

"I'm here to pick up an application to become a state trooper," I said.

He looked at me strangely and I thought there had to be something wrong. Was my slip showing or a button open on my blouse? I glanced around the room for a mirror, but there was none.

"Are you Marilyn Derubio?" the trooper asked.

"Yes," I said.

"You'll have to go to the state campus to pick up your application."

"The campus?" I asked. The campus is a complex of state office buildings in Albany. "I called ahead and was told to come here."

"I know," he said. "It was a mistake." He leaned on his desk and drew a diagram of the campus. Next to him I felt small and out of place.

"You're to see Mr. MacNamara," he said.

As I drove to the campus, I saw it was one of those rare, perfect spring mornings, where puffy white clouds slipped across the sky. I was young, just out of school, and excited about the prospect of a career in law enforcement. It was a day that could have become the happiest day of my life, and yet something was wrong. On the way to the barracks I was singing along with the radio. Now, as I drove to the state campus, I was subtly aware that my mood had been shattered by the brief encounter with the state trooper.

I was still somewhat bewildered and nervous as I entered the state office building. I took the elevator all the way to the top so that I could be alone long enough to pat down my skirt, check the buttons on my blouse, and assess my makeup in a compact mirror; then I went down to Mr. MacNamara's office.

There was a sign on the open door that said, "Public Relations." I glanced in. A man was sitting at a desk looking at some papers. The placard said, "Walter MacNamara, Public Relations."

This isn't right. I'm in the wrong place, I thought, wondering where I would find the right Mr. MacNamara. I started to turn. Mr. MacNamara looked up.

"Come in, come in, dear," he called cheerfully. He stood up. He was an older, ruddy-faced man, silver-haired and recklessly overweight. He seemed to waddle as he stepped around his desk and came across the room. He slipped an arm around me as if I were his niece.

"Sorry about the confusion," he said, "but you're here now. Marilyn, is it?"

"Yes," I said, "Marilyn Derubio."

"Derubio? You're Italian, huh?"

"And Irish," I said.

His desk was one of those gun-metal gray monsters that seem to darken any room.

"Have a seat, have a seat," Mr. MacNamara said. He went back around his desk, plopped into a swivel chair, and looked at me. Suddenly the smile, which he had worn since my arrival, drained from his face, and now he stared across his desk at me with a look of disapproval.

"So," he finally said, "you want to be a police officer."

Somehow he made it sound as if he were talking to a five-year-old girl.

"Yes," I said.

"Why?" he snapped.

"Because I think I'd be good at it," I stammered.

"I see," he said. "You think you'd be good at it. How old are you, seventeen?"

"Eighteen," I said. "I've already graduated from high school."

"Eighteen and you think you'd be good at it," he said somewhat sarcastically, but with a smile.

"Yes," I said again.

"Young lady, do you know what's going on in the world?" he asked.

"Excuse me?" I asked, not quite understanding why the conversation was going the way it was.

"There is a war in Vietnam, and communists are over here organizing riots," he said. "There are long-haired kids throwing paint at cops, calling them pigs—taking over college campuses like a bunch of criminals. Do you think a gal like you could handle these drugged-up hippies coming at you, spitting at you?" he asked.

"I'd do my best sir," I said.

For a long time Mr. MacNamara looked straight into my eyes.

"The flag burners would eat you for lunch," he said.

I said nothing.

"You're not going to meet the minimum weight requirement of one hundred and sixty pounds," he said.

"I'm healthy," I said. "I can pass a physical."

"And you're certainly not five-foot-ten," he added, as if I hadn't spoken.

"I've only come for an application, and not many women are five-foot, ten-inches tall and one hundred and sixty pounds. I don't think height is an important job qualification," I said.

"You don't, huh? Well, it is," he said. He stared at me

with his watery gray eyes, then he leaned forward. "Let me tell you something, young lady. There has never been a woman state trooper in New York State and there never will be. It's not a woman's job."

I was absolutely in shock. With a single statement he had shattered a dream that I had carried with me for most of my life. I couldn't even speak. I was numb.

As Mr. MacNamara led me out of his office, he said, "Believe me, I've been at this for forty years; it's no life for a woman."

I cringed under the touch of his hand on my shoulder.

"The pay's lousy," he was saying, "the hours are murder." But all I could think was that I wasn't even being given a chance. I was being rejected for no reason, except that I was female. I didn't think about appeals or lawsuits or anything like that. He said there would be no female troopers and I accepted it.

"I haven't always been behind a desk, you know," he said. "No, sir, I did my time in the ranks. Believe me, it's no picnic day at the beach. You'll do well at something else."

I left the building and drove home feeling helpless and crushed. I didn't even get the application.

My other dream when I was eighteen was to be a wife and mother.

Within two years of that heartbreaking day in Walter MacNamara's office, I had gotten married to my high-school sweetheart, given birth to a beautiful baby boy, and watched my young husband march off to war in Vietnam.

Since my parents were nearby to care for the baby during the day, I took a job as a receptionist and telephone operator at Wallberg Electric Supply Company.

I often regretted not having a career in law enforcement, but deep down I knew that it had not been what I really wanted, not exactly.

What I really wanted was to find missing people. Since

childhood I had been fascinated by the idea. It had never occurred to me that a person could make a career of such a thing, so I had gravitated toward law enforcement, thinking that it would be as close as I would ever come to looking for missing people. The truth is, I never really had much interest in handing out speeding tickets.

Before going to work at Wallberg in the morning, I would search the newspapers for stories about people who had never come home or who had left for work and never arrived. Later, as I went about the mundane chores of motherhood—changing diapers for my new baby, heating formula, rocking baby Paul to sleep—I would think about the missing-persons cases, turning them in my mind like unusual stones, examining each tantalizing facet for a clue. Where did he go? Why did he go? What happened? How could he be found?

Often I fantasized about being called in on a missing-person case and somehow solving a mystery that no one else had been able to solve: "Marilyn, this is the New York State Police. We're really stymied on this one, and we were wondering if you could come in and help us out with it."

When my husband, Brad, came back from Vietnam, I quit my job at Wallberg, thinking I could devote full time to my baby and the apartment we lived in. But things had changed.

When Brad had gone off to war he was young and good-natured. When he came back he was a man, but a broken and tortured man, prone to fits of temper and deep brooding depression that sometimes brought him to the brink of suicide. I knew within days of his return that our marriage was doomed. They had taken away my sweet young husband and sent back a monster. Brad was moody. He was violent. He couldn't hold onto a job. He frightened me. It was only a matter of months before his fits of temper led us to divorce.

After my divorce I went back to work at Wallberg as a cashier. It was there that I met Chip Greene. Chip was a counterman, and my cash register was at the end of the counter, so we worked closely together all day. I didn't care for Chip at first. He was loud and raucous, and he made any room he entered sound like a men's locker room. But also he made me giggle at a time when that counted for quite a lot. We shared a sense of humor, and conversation flowed easily between us. He brought me a flower. We started dating.

On our first date Chip took me to a restaurant where I ordered lobster, which I had never had in my life. It was expensive, but Chip insisted that if lobster was what I wanted, lobster was what I should get.

We sat in a small corner booth with the shadows from an electric candle dancing across our faces. Chip reached across the table and touched my fingers lightly.

"So tell me about the missing people," he said.

"What missing people?"

"You told me once that you were interested in missing people. Tell me about that."

"I'm surprised you remembered," I said. My interest in missing people had been mostly part of my inner life. I wasn't used to people asking me about it. I was pleased.

I began with a story from my childhood. Although I had spent most of my life in the Albany area, there had been a few years in my childhood when my parents and my brother and I lived in California. We were a working-class family, and my father had taken us out there hoping to get better pay. It was then that I became interested in missing people.

I told Chip that, when I was a child in Burbank, a lot of little girls disappeared and several were found dead. The police warned children not to go anywhere with strangers. The disappearances were on the front page of the paper every day and on the TV news every evening. One day during the height of the hysteria, my girlfriend Linda and I walked through an alley behind a restaurant and came across a deep hole where water from a leaky pipe had worn away the concrete surface of the alley. We stared down into the hole and saw a dead cat. Linda jumped back and let out a shriek that must have carried all the way to Anaheim. Of course, everybody in town was on edge, so dozens of people came running. Police cars sped to the scene with sirens wailing. Policemen on motorcycles came roaring into the alley. It was as if an entire SWAT team had instantly been dropped in by helicopter. "They'll think I did it," Linda said. She turned and ran like the dickens. But I wasn't afraid. I stayed to show the police the horrible thing we had found.

During this same period a neighborhood girl named Heather disappeared one morning. Everybody was frantic. All day long police cars with loudspeakers cruised up and down the streets, calling, "Heather, come out if you can hear me."

Without telling anybody, I decided to help in the search. I walked around the neighborhood, staring up into trees, looking behind houses, under bushes, each time thinking I would discover the little girl and she would be fine and I would return her to her parents.

At three o'clock that afternoon the police found Heather. She had wandered into a neighbor's garage where she had climbed way up on a high shelf in the back and gone to sleep on a rug. It fascinated me to know that a person could be right in the middle of a search area and not be found.

When I finished talking, Chip asked me what it was that attracted me to a missing-person case.

"I don't know," I said. "It's like a puzzle, and I want to solve it."

Chip and I dated often, and often I talked about missing people. Chip seemed interested, though, I guess like most people, he thought that the disappearance of strangers was a curious thing to be interested in.

Neither Chip nor I were impetuous, so our romance was neither fast nor fiery. But in time we were married, and after we had saved some money Chip announced that he wanted to move out of our Albany apartment to Berne, south of Albany, where he had grown up.

Berne is the proverbial town in the middle of nowhere, and I wanted to move there as much as I wanted to undergo root-canal work, but I was very influenced by my father's thinking then: "He's your husband, Marilyn, and if that's where he wants to move, then you go with him. You have no right to tell your husband where he can and cannot live."

So we moved to Berne, to a small farmhouse in an area so desolate it could have been on Jupiter. I had a neighbor on my left and a neighbor on my right, and beyond their houses stretched miles of meadow and woodland where no one lived but the wildlife. There were few playmates for my son, Paul, so he spent a lot of time alone. Being so far from the city, he no longer had his grandparents to play with every day, and the sadness often showed on his face.

My relationship with Chip changed. Now he had two hours of commuting each day, and there was no way he could pop in for lunch. Chip went to classes two nights a week, he went bowling two nights a week, and he worked late one night a week. Most nights he would get home at nine o'clock, eat, and go to bed. At six-thirty the next morning I was once again alone with a preschooler. I was sick with loneliness.

Paul was the bright spot in my life. This was a time of great explorations and magnificent discoveries for a two-year-old boy in a new house. And, of course, it was a time for me to put everything breakable or harmful high on a shelf or in a locked drawer. When Paul did manage to yank on something that I shouldn't have left dangling, he would let out a howl and I would come running and scoop him into my arms. It felt wonderful to be needed.

Paul was great. But he wasn't enough. I desperately craved something else, something that would give me an identity of my own. At night I dreamed of doing something more important than waxing the kitchen floor. I knew I was in trouble when I found myself in the kitchen one morning, staring into a cup of coffee and wondering if I really existed or if I only imagined that I existed. Marilyn, I thought, better get yourself a hobby.

The one thing that did capture my attention at this time was the search for a boy named Douglas Legg. Douglas had disappeared in the Adirondack Mountains, and a trained search team had flown in from Seattle, Washington, to look for him because there were no such search teams in our area. I was fascinated by the fact that the Seattle search team was small and worked with air-scent dogs. Each morning I read the newspaper accounts with such concern that anybody would think the boy was in my family. They never found Douglas Legg, but more than ever I knew that searching for a boy like that was something I could really develop an interest in.

A few weeks later, Chip and I were watching the eleven o'clock news. We had fought over some small matter and, though our chairs were only feet apart, there were miles between us. He was weary from work and night school. I was weary from housework and motherhood. Somehow in the crush of daily life the spark between us had been extinguished. I felt lonely and worthless. I remember looking at him and thinking, I married this man, and yet we hardly know each other.

"Three small children are lost in the Adirondack woods tonight," the anchorman said. "Billy Joe Taylor, age two, is missing, along with his brother William, age three, and their sister Lisa Jane, age four. The children are from Ticonderoga. Police have issued a call for volunteers to help in the search."

I dashed to the small desk in the living room, grabbed a pencil, and started jotting down the details.

At first I thought, you can't go, what would you do? I went to bed. After an hour of sleeplessness I knew what I had to do. I got up, dressed warmly, then woke up Chip.

"I'm going to go," I said.

"Go where?" Chip asked. "What are you talking about?"

"Ticonderoga."

"For what?"

"Didn't you hear? They're looking for volunteers to help find those kids."

"They're not looking for you, Marilyn. They're looking for men to go out there."

I was halfway into the kitchen. "Women search, too," I said. I scooped up my car keys and put on my coat.

"Are you crazy?" Chip said. "It's one o'clock in the morning and it's twenty degrees out there."

"That's why they have to find those kids tonight," I said. "They'll die in this cold. I can't sleep knowing that."

"Marilyn, you're being ridiculous."

"No. I'm not." I was halfway to the door. "Isn't it great?"

"Great? You think it's great that you're going off into the night like a crazy person?"

"No," I said, as I walked into the cold night air. "I think it's great that I want to go. I went to bed every night of the Douglas Legg search. I'm not going to do that again."

At three o'clock in the morning I pulled in behind a row of trucks and state-police cars with their lights rotating and their radios crackling. Wisps of steam rose from a coffee urn that had been mounted on one of the police cars. Three men in long winter jackets surrounded the urn, warming their hands against Styrofoam cups filled with black coffee. The temperature had dropped to below fifteen degrees.

Ticonderoga is a beautiful area of deep green hills between Lake George and Lake Champlain. In the summer it is booming with tourists from all over New York and Canada. Then there is a slow period during fall when residents get the opportunity to relax before the ski season begins with the first snowfall. It was now fall, and luckily there were many area residents available to help with this search.

One of the men at the coffee urn directed me to the state trooper who was in charge of the search.

The trooper, leaning over the trunk of his cruiser and running his fingers over a map, was built like the door to a vault. As I approached him, my skin suddenly felt as thin as paper. I remembered Chip's words: "They're not looking for you, Marilyn. They're looking for men to go out there."

"I came to help in the search," I said.

He glanced up from the map. "Thanks for coming," he said. "We're looking for three lost children. The oldest is four years old. They're not dressed for this weather. We have to find them tonight."

I went back to my car for a flashlight, and when I returned he took me behind the house where the children lived. It was an extraordinary sight. Dozens of flashlights cut across the dark night sky. I stared at them through the haze of my own breath floating before me in the cold night air.

Those lights dancing across the mountain before me were a reminder that our noblest quality as human beings is that we try to help each other. Many of the people holding those flashlights did not know the missing children, but they had compassion enough to come out in the middle of a cold night to help.

The area behind the children's house was level ground for only about twenty feet. Then it dropped off sharply for about fifty or seventy-five feet through thick briars to a small creek. I looked at the drop-off with my light. I could see rusted cans, papers, and bottles under the briars where burning barrels had been emptied over the edge. The drop-off was steep too. Getting down to the creek would require a searcher to take good notice of his footing and hang onto the branches that didn't have thorns on them.

On the other side of the creek, the land angled sharply up again and was equally covered with short thorn bushes. As my eyes adjusted to the dark I could see the searchers now, not just their flashlight beams on the mountainside. They were moving slowly and carefully, as the terrain was treacherously steep.

With the beam of his flashlight the trooper marked off an area for me to search, then he went back to his car.

I slid down to the creek, crossed over, then climbed the mountain on the other side. There were no trails or easy paths, so I had to push through the thorn bushes most of the way.

I knew instantly that we were all doing something futile. We were looking for a two-year-old boy on a mountain that no two-year-old could climb.

As I moved back and forth across the slope in long lines parallel to the creek, I wondered if these people knew they were wasting precious time looking in a place where the children couldn't be.

Finally, I thought, Marilyn, this is not right, and I edged my way down the hill and returned to the state trooper.

"Officer," I said, "I have a two-year-old son of my own, and I'm certain he couldn't climb a slope like that."

The trooper didn't say anything. He just looked at me and nodded his head as if he expected me to continue.

"Also," I said, "it seems likely that the three children would stay together."

"Probably," he said.

"And their travel would be limited to the capabilities of the smallest child."

"Yes," he said. He seemed to be genuinely interested in what I had to say.

"If I were to bring my two-year-old son here and let him go, he'd go over there." I pointed to the flat wooded area across the street from the house. There was a truck road leading into it, with deep tire ruts and a hump in the middle.

"Already thought of that," the trooper said.

I felt my cheeks grow hot with embarrassment. Of course they've already thought of that, Marilyn, they're not idiots.

"And we searched that road several times," he added. "They're not there."

"Oh," I said. I felt foolish. I turned on my flashlight and drifted toward the back of the house again.

"And, miss," the trooper called to me.

"Yes," I said.

"You're right. Those little kids can't climb that mountain. But after you've been on a few searches, you'll find that missing people have a way of ending up in places they can't possibly be. Don't rule out any place until you've looked."

I smiled at him. "What makes you think I'll be on more searches?"

"You will," he said.

I went back to my assigned area and climbed up the slope to the place where I had been. But the flashlight just hung limp in my hand. Okay, I thought, maybe someday three very small children will work their way up a mountain like this and someone like me will be wrong. But it's not this night and it's not these kids and it's not this mountain. I was sure of it.

After I finished searching my assigned area, I worked my way back to the front of the house. More state-police cars had arrived, along with a canteen truck and an ambulance. I got a cup of coffee at the canteen truck and as I stood there with two other searchers, talking about the heartless cold that was on everybody's mind, I kept glancing at the truck road on the other side of the street. What the heck, I thought, so they searched it. It wouldn't hurt to search it again.

With my flashlight in my hand I went across the street and walked into the woods. The meandering road was covered with pine needles. It was soft beneath my feet, and each time I took a step the pine needles crackled in the darkness and I stopped, thinking I had heard a child's cry. I swept my flashlight beam back and forth across the road. On both sides were thick tangled bushes, winter-bare but still dense enough to hide lost children.

I moved forward on the road, pushing my light deeper into the woods.

After ten minutes of walking, methodically sweeping my flashlight from side to side, I heard a sound. I stopped. I heard it again, and then again, but the sound slid off into the distance. It was the sound of some nocturnal creature scurrying about in the dark. I began walking again and, in the dark, about fifty feet ahead of me and moving toward me, I saw the shadowy outline of a creature about the size of a bear.

I froze on the spot. I wasn't really afraid, but I was acutely aware of just how vulnerable we are, alone in the woods. There are no phones to reach for, no fire alarms to yank, no one even to hear our shouts when the weather, or the lack of food, or something dangerous threatens our lives. As the large creature lumbered into the circle of light that I cast ahead of me, I saw that it was no more than a man, a tall, strapping young man with a beard that hung down to his chest. As he moved slowly closer I could see that the reason he looked so immense in the shadows was that he was carrying two little boys, one locked securely in each arm. The four-year-old little girl trailed behind him, clinging to his coat as though afraid of being left behind.

"You found them," I said.

"Ay," he said, "just by accident." He had a strong French-Canadian accent. When he got close to me he handed over the smaller boy and picked up the girl and snuggled her against him to warm her body. "I was walking down this road, ay," he said—as I led us along with my flashlight in one hand, the sleeping boy held tightly in my other arm—"and I saw this bush with a little patch of white sticking out amongst the leaves, ay. I touched it and these three jumped up in a puff of steam, ay. These little rascals must have got tired and just piled themselves over with leaves and went to sleep, ay. The searchers have been up and down here a dozen times, ay."

We walked out of the woods to the surprise and relief of everyone. I felt a sense of accomplishment about my participation in the search, although I knew I had nothing to do with finding the kids. The children were safe. That was the important thing.

By the time I got back to the farmhouse in Berne the sun was up. The ride home had been long. It gave me time to think.

Sleeping children covered with leaves, I thought. Searchers must have walked right by them. A dog wouldn't have missed them. A dog could have shortened the search.

Pulling up to the house I felt that it didn't look quite as isolated as it had, and the world around me looked clearer. The trees, the hills, the clouds, everything seemed to be more sharply etched against the morning sky. I felt good. I felt valuable. I hadn't found the children but I had been part of the finding. For now, that was enough.

2

"I want to be in search-and-rescue because I think it would be, I don't know, just great, you know, to find someone's lost little boy," the girl said. I don't remember her name. Michelle, I think. She was a pretty young woman, twenty-one or so, with honey-colored hair and more makeup than she needed. I was only a few years older, but I envied her freedom. It was night and we were in the cramped living room of a small suburban house in Utica. A dozen of us, mostly men, had responded to a newspaper item that said a search-and-rescue team was being formed to serve New York State. Sitting in a circle, we were taking turns telling the group why we wanted to be part of a search-and-rescue team. Michelle was wearing a black miniskirt and white go-go boots. I remember thinking, she doesn't belong here. And then wondering, Do I belong here?

This was about a month after the Ticonderoga search. During that time I had thought often about those three children. Just how close had they come to not being found, I wondered. What if there hadn't been a little white patch sticking out among the leaves?

I had thought often about my own life, too. I had taken a job as a clerk-typist, but it was mindless work, no more fulfilling than scrubbing the bathroom floor. I still needed something else, and when I saw the newspaper item about the search-and-rescue team, I jumped at it. Of course I had no time. I had a son, a husband, a house, and a job. But I drove to that meeting full of excitement.

When the meeting ended that night, I knew Michelle

and a few others would never be back. I knew that I would. I became a founding member of Adirondack Search and Rescue, along with Don Arner, publisher of *Off Lead* magazine, and Richard Dennis, a carpenter. In the weeks that followed, the three of us spoke often with Bill Syrotuck, the nationally known S-and-R expert who had flown his team in from Seattle to search for Douglas Legg. As the organization grew we occasionally flew Bill and his wife, Jean, in from Seattle to help in our training.

As with any group, there was a knot of organizational problems, clashing egos, and shallow motives to be untangled. Many people were attracted to search-and-rescue for the wrong reasons. They wanted to be the hero who carried the little boy safely out of the woods. We all wanted that, but as we went along, learning from experts and largely teaching ourselves, we realized that the tragic truth is that the person who is the subject of an extended search is more often dead than alive. Some people lost interest in a hurry when that fact became clear to them, so the early meetings were a culling process. This was serious. A bowling team can survive despite wishy-washy members and frequent dropouts. A search-and-rescue team cannot.

Although in some ways S-and-R was our hobby, we also knew that we were into some pretty serious business; and right from the start it was important to sort out those people who would lose interest the first time their phone rang at two o'clock in the morning and they were told to be at the airport in an hour. Our need to sift out these people was one of the main reasons we decided to camp out overnight for our training meetings.

After the first weekend meeting was scheduled, I began to get cold feet. I wasn't afraid of sleeping outdoors. I was afraid of telling Chip. Chip worked hard all week, and he liked to go fishing with his friend Gizzo on the weekends. How could I ask him to spend a weekend at home alone taking care of Paul, cooking for himself, especially since he had very graciously taken care of Paul while I was attending organizational meetings? Of course I worked hard all week, too. But, still, it didn't seem right to ask this of Chip. And yet, I wanted to be part of search-and-rescue more than I wanted anything.

I put off telling Chip for as long as I dared, which wasn't difficult, since I hardly ever saw him. But the delay only built up the problem in my mind. By the Thursday night before the first training weekend I was a nervous wreck. I put a roast in the oven, then I fed Paul early so that Chip and I could eat a quiet supper alone.

I'd been learning a lot about the air-scent dogs that were used for searches in Europe but were practically unknown in the United States. I was excited about what I was learning, and I thought that if I could get Chip as enthusiastic as I was, he would understand about the training weekend.

When Chip got home he was in one of his quiet moods. This was unnerving because it was difficult to read him. We sat down to supper, Chip with his head down as if he were reading a newspaper.

"How was work?" I asked.

"The usual," he said, not looking up.

I could hear the ticking of the small clock that sat on top of the refrigerator, and in that old farmhouse kitchen the creak of every little movement we made was a reminder of just how silent things had become. My dog, Saki, sat quietly by the door, now and then pushing his nose through the air in the direction of the food on our plates.

"Meat okay?" I asked.

"Fine."

I didn't want to start right in on my search-and-rescue stuff. I waited for Chip to talk, to ask about my day, about Paul, something. But there was nothing. The silence was like an itch that needed to be scratched.

"I've been learning a lot about the air-scent dogs," I finally said. "They're amazing animals. In Europe they use them to find people who are buried in avalanches. They can find people who are buried under twenty feet of snow."

"What type of dog?" Chip asked, cutting into his beef.

"Air-scent," I said. I could hear the nervousness in my voice. "They're not really a type. It's the way the dog is trained."

"Really? They train French poodles for this sort of thing, do they?"

Chip looked up now. He was smiling. I couldn't tell whether he was playing with me or making fun of me. I hoped he'd still be smiling after I told him I was going away for the weekend.

"No," I said, laughing. "No poodles. German shepherds mostly. Like Saki."

"So what do you do, give them a glove to sniff?"

"No. Al Romeo says they don't need any scent object."

"Al Romeo? Who the hell is Al Romeo?"

"You know. He's on my search-and-rescue team. He knows a lot about the dogs."

"Oh."

"See, all people emit a scent that is caused by the millions of dead skin cells shed by the body every minute. Even the slightest of air currents carries the scent away, downwind, just like smoke. The scent forms a cone shape. It's strong and narrow near the lost person, then grows wide and more sparse the farther away the wind carries it."

"I thought you told me that many of these people would be dead before you even got an opportunity to look for them," Chip said.

"Well, that's true. But it doesn't affect the scent cone. The dog can still find them just as quickly," I said.

"How does the dog know who he's looking for?"

"The dogs are not trained to discriminate scents because many times there isn't an article from the missing person available or searchers may not have a starting point from which to run a trail. So they will find every human who is in a given area," I said.

"But that's okay. It means that the dog can be used after ground searchers have gone through the area, and they will also be just as effective after rain, snow, or the passage of a few days," I added.

"Why are you telling me about these dogs?" Chip asked.

"I thought you'd be interested."

"I am interested. But there's more to it than that. You're telling me for a reason. What is it?"

"I want to train Saki," I said.

"So, go ahead. He's your dog. What's the problem?"

"I have to go away this weekend to Utica. That's where we'll be training." There, I had said it. I could feel my pulse throbbing. "It's an overnight camping trip. I won't leave until Saturday morning and I'll be back Sunday night, I promise."

"I see," Chip said. His words were like two ice cubes being dropped on the table.

I could have told Chip that it takes a long time to train a dog and that I would have to go away for a weekend every month, but I didn't tell him. I wanted to handle one crisis at a time. I could feel the tension descend on the room. The Adirondack Search and Rescue meetings had already been a difficult subject for the two of us.

On Saturday morning I crept out of bed at four o'clock. It was still dark out, and as I tiptoed about the house I felt at once exhilarated and lonely. I was embarking on a great adventure in my life, but I felt as if I had no one at home with whom to share it.

I had already made arrangements for a baby-sitter to come in during the hours when Chip would not be home. And now, as I prepared and wrapped several small meals for Paul and sliced up potatoes and carrots which I poured into the slow cooker for Chip's stew, I told myself I was doing my best for my family. But there was a critical voice inside me that produced feelings of guilt. Marilyn, it said, you're a wife, a mother; do you really have the time to devote to search-and-rescue? Suppressing the thought, I loaded the car with camping gear and Saki before I went into Paul's room to kiss him goodbye.

Paul was awake. He looked frightened. On Friday night I had read him a story about a bear that went to Paris, and I had explained to him that where I was going was not nearly as far as Paris. But, still, I had never left him for a weekend before, and I wasn't surprised when he became weepy and worried.

"Well, hon, I'm off to Utica," I said now. I reached to pat his sad little face. Tears came into his eyes again and he turned his face into the pillow.

"Oh, Paul, I'll be home tomorrow. Today you'll have Daddy all to yourself."

Paul didn't answer. I couldn't hear his sobs, but I could see his little body heaving up and down slightly as he cried into his pillow. For a moment I thought, the hell with it, I won't go. I'll stay here with my son and husband. But I knew that if I stayed and gave up this one thing in my life, I would forever be staring at the door and wondering what might have been. I kissed the back of Paul's head. "Love you," I said, and I hurried out of the house before I could change my mind.

The drive to Utica, once I pushed worries about Paul and Chip from my mind, was a pleasure. We had chosen Utica, a medium-sized city on the Mohawk River, because team members would be coming from Rochester as well as the Albany area. Now, as I drove the eighty-five miles north to our rendezvous, I could see that the area was perfect for other reasons. Spring was still fresh, and the rolling green hills that rose around me as I drove up the New York State Thruway renewed my sense of exhilaration for my new project. I was surrounded by a patchwork of dairy farms and mustard-colored meadows. Beyond them were thick woods, only now beginning to fill with green. Utica was nestled in the Mohawk Valley between the Adirondack and Catskill mountains. The area had the variety of terrain we would need to train ourselves properly for all situations.

We began in a wide meadow south of the city, six of us and our dogs, each knowing something, none of us knowing it all. We knew that searching with the air-scent dogs would not be unique but it would be unusual in the United States. The traditional method of searching for a lost person in the wilderness is the grid search, made up of grid lines. A grid line consists of a group of people assembled in a straight line, moving in one direction as they search for the missing person or evidence.

The grid has been used for years, but it does have drawbacks. When you cram 300 or 400 people into one square mile of search area you sometimes create administrative nightmares. An overzealous searcher will spot the victim, only to have it turn out to be another searcher. Many searchers assume that other searchers have swept through a particular area when they have not. If you want to space people ten feet apart for a mile you have to get 528 people, which often is more than the entire population of the nearest town. Then you need a place for them to park, and you have to feed them and communicate with them, and when the search is all over you have to go back in and find the 3 or 4 searchers who got lost. The probability of finding the victim remains high only if the 528 people are extremely well organized.

But we hadn't started Adirondack Search and Rescue to conduct grid searches. Our primary search tool right from the beginning was the air-scent dog, and the training of the dogs was the most important activity of the training weekends.

We learned a lot about the dogs from Al Romeo. Not quite forty, Al had already served twenty years in the air force and had retired on a livable pension. Most of his time was spent on volunteer work. He was a part-time ambulance driver, a member of one other rescue organization, and a church organist. Al had three German shepherds, and one, Lackland, came with him on the Utica weekends.

On that first Saturday we all sat in a circle in the grass and Al told us about the air-scent dogs. He explained that the dogs were to be worked "off lead." That is, they could move on their own within sight of the handler, in a pattern determined by the handler. "In the wilderness it is not unusual for an experienced dog-and-handler team to detect a scent a half mile from the subject," he said. "The record is over two miles, during a search in Alaska."

Al warned us right from the beginning that it would take well over a year to train the dogs.

In Utica we trained our dogs on a play-reward system. I began by giving Saki a ball to retrieve. Once he became an enthusiastic retriever, it was time for the next training step. He had to find me.

On my third weekend in Utica, Al stayed with Saki on a leash in an open hilly area where there was a stream to one side and a small stand of trees to the other. I walked over a hill and went about a hundred yards before I slipped into the woods.

Then Al let Saki off lead. "Go find," he called. Saki raised his nose and sampled the air.

"Go find," Al said again, and Saki darted off.

"That's it, go find," Al said. "Go find." When Al could see that Saki recognized the scent, he called out more enthusiastically, "That's it, go boy, go find her." It took Saki twenty minutes to cover the small distance. There was a lot of zigging and zagging, a lot of sniffing the air to find the scent again. But finally he found me. He stared at me and wagged his tail happily. I found a stick in order to reward him with a session of play.

The dogs usually performed well, and when they did, Al would shout, "Good boy, you found her." Al reminded me that even though the moment of discovery would sometimes be a painful one for the handler, the dog must be shown that he had done something good, and the congratulatory words would have to be delivered in a happy and positive tone of voice, no matter how grim the discovery.

One weekend a month would never be enough to train an air-scent dog. I put Saki through sessions like this three times a week at home, until he clearly understood the command "Go find." In Utica I gradually advanced Saki from finding me to finding Al or one of the other team members. At home I sent him in search of Paul, or my neighbor Jennifer, or whoever was willing to hide in the woods while Saki sniffed the air.

I loved the training weekends. We slept in tents in summer heat and winter cold. The campfire was our kitchen, the woods were our bathroom, and for twelve hours a day we worked with our dogs, urging them to find fellow rescuers who were hiding up in trees, behind rocks, or under mounds of snow.

What I did not love was shoehorning these weekends into my life. Before each weekend I would prepare meals, arrange for baby-sitters, pack my gear, and listen to grumbling about how I was deserting my family. Paul, more than Chip, was determined to sabotage my trips. He would whine, break things, act out, do whatever he thought would keep Mommy home. Of course, the loudest grumbling would come not from my son or my husband but from my own conscience, and so along with my camping equipment I would invariably carry a heavy load of guilt to Utica.

From time to time new people joined ASAR and we were pleased to have them. Everyone was welcome, but the training weekends were effective in weeding out those who were not ready or truly willing. There was one seventy-six-year-old man who had come to all the early meetings, and he actually made it to Utica three times. He was a dear, and more than anything he wanted to be useful. But he was slow and ill, and the idea of his spending twelve hours a day hiking through a wilderness area was ludicrous.

And I remember one woman, Clara Winokur, who had gotten tired of watching her husband, Tom, drive off to Utica one weekend every month. She joined ASAR so she could spend the weekends with him. On Saturday night I sat with her by the campfire.

"You know, this is really the life, isn't it?" she said, checking her makeup in a small compact mirror. "I mean, look at those stars."

I leaned back and stared up at the heavens. It was always a sight so riveting that often I wanted to stay awake all night and gaze at the sky. In the wilderness you can see ten times as many stars as you can see in the city, where air pollution and electric lights dilute the spectacular effect. Out there the silver is brighter, the black is blacker, and the stars shine like diamonds spilled across an endless velvet cloak.

"And the air is so fresh," Clara said, "and everything is so quiet." She took a deep, contented breath. "This is just great."

On Sunday morning I found her sitting on a rock, with a depressed look on her face. Dark lines circled her eyes, and her hair looked as if somebody had gone through it with an eggbeater.

"How was your night?" I asked.

"Awful," she said. Her hands were trembling. She looked like a woman who would kill for a bubble bath or a shampoo and set. "I was awake all night. I was terrified. How can you sleep with all these . . . animals around?"

"Animals?"

"Yes. My god, there was some kind of predatory bird circling around our tent half the night. I thought it was going to claw its way in. Finally it did whatever those things do, and I heard it catch another animal right outside the tent, and then the thing carried its victim off. I could hear the wings flapping. It was horrible. I still haven't gone to the bathroom."

That was Clara's last trip to Utica.

By the time the dogs were trained, I had been elected president of Adirondack Search and Rescue. The honor was somewhat dubious because I was awarded it primarily for my secretarial skills.

The president was the one who got calls in the middle of the night from state-police or sheriffs' departments asking ASAR to help search for a lost person. I learned very quickly that the spirit of cooperation between rescue volunteers and law-enforcement agencies was absent as often as it was present. Our early searches were often successful in spite of the police, not because of them.

In one case, I was called by the sheriff of an upstate–New York county who wanted us to search for a man by the name of Michael Trahan.

"We really need help on this one," he said. "The man's been missing for two weeks."

I told the sheriff I'd be glad to get some volunteers together and we would come up. I organized a small team, and early that Saturday morning we drove 150 miles to the site with our dogs.

Michael Trahan was a middle-aged man who lived in a suburban area. Several hundred acres of woods formed a crescent around his neighborhood, and he had gone there often to be alone. For some time he had been emotionally troubled, and one day he had simply wandered off. He hadn't taken a car, and there was no evidence that he had left town. It was winter, and two weeks had gone by. If he had gotten lost in those woods, he almost certainly was dead.

The other members of the team and I worked separate areas of the woods for one long cold day. For hours the dogs wandered through the area without showing any sign of catching a scent. Finally, late in the afternoon when the light in the woods was fading quickly, Don Wendell's dog went on strong alert.

When an air-scent dog smells something, he alerts. His head goes up, his body stiffens, and he begins to move forward in a very purposeful way. You don't have to be an expert to know when a dog is alerting. You can see that he is no longer just searching; he has direction.

Don's dog chased the scent across an open field and into a gulley, then he galloped back and bounded off Don's chest, which usually means, "I've found him, I've found him." We followed the dog but found no sign of a man. We continued to work the area with the dogs, but none of them found a scent. We gave up at the end of the day. I drove home, feeling sad that we had not been called in as soon as the man had disappeared. I felt he must be dead, but I couldn't get it out of my mind that there had been somebody in that field. Either the wind may have changed in such a way that it never again carried the scent to the dogs, or somebody may have moved, evading the searchers.

Two months went by. There were other searches, and I didn't know whether Trahan had been found until I got another call from the sheriff, telling me that the man was still missing and the family was pressing hard for some action. He asked me if I would come up again and coordinate a search. I told him I would, and it was agreed that the county would reimburse the gas, tolls, and phone expenses.

"No problem," the sheriff said. "We can take care of that." There was a pause, and then he asked, "You're not going to bring your dogs, are you?"

"No," I said. "Too much time has gone by."

"Good," he said. "Look forward to seeing you."

The day before the search was to take place I called Dave Onderdonk, a bloodhound handler I knew who lived in Rensselaer, New York. I wanted to find Trahan, though I thought he was probably dead. I asked Dave if his team would join the search in the morning. He said they would, and by the time we got off the phone we agreed that it wouldn't hurt for Dave to drive down to the search area that night and give it one last try with his dog.

Almost from the beginning Dave's dog ran a hot trail. But it didn't make much sense. The dog ran east, then he ran west, then east again—then south. The dog was on constant alert.

Dave urged the dog on. "Good girl, go find him, good girl, good girl."

Even though the dog was looping all over the woods and fields, Dave had to assume the dog was on to something. Dogs alert for a reason. There seemed to be two possibilities. Either several people were in the woods in the middle of the night or one person was moving around.

Dave worked the dog for several hours, and the dog's alerts were aimed at a narrower and narrower area. The dog was closing in on something. At two o'clock in the morning, when Dave's flashlight batteries were starting to weaken and he was getting weary, the dog led him out of the woods. He followed his dog into the nearby neighborhood. It seemed insane, but the dog was still alerting and Dave trusted the animal. Still the dog kept moving. "Good girl, good girl, go find him, good girl," Dave called along the dark and empty streets.

The dog led him to the back door of a house—Michael Trahan's house.

For a short time Dave stood out in the cold night air staring at the house and wondering what to do next. It was all very mysterious. He waited. The dog sniffed around the house and returned to Dave, then sniffed some more. Dave knocked on the door. Lights came on and Dave heard movement in the house. Finally, a woman, Michael Trahan's mother, came to the door in her nightgown. She looked at Dave, then she glanced to her side and let out a tremendous shriek. Then Dave heard several loud thuds. It was the sound of Michael Trahan tumbling down the cellar stairs.

It turned out that Michael Trahan was severely mentally ill. He had been hiding in the woods during the day and sneaking back into his own home late at night to get food and sleep in a crawl space in the cellar. Dave's dog had chased him back toward the house. When his mother opened the door she had seen him pressed against a wall at the entrance to the cellar.

I was thrilled when Dave called to tell me all of this. He had found the man alive, and we could call off the grid search.

"But there's something wrong," Dave said. "The police have been real cold to me. I thought they might take me out and buy me a cup of coffee. Instead I'm getting the cold shoulder. I don't need praise, but a thank-you would be nice."

I didn't know what was going on. I just congratulated Dave for a good job and later I sent the department receipts for about ninety dollars, mostly for gas and long-distance phone calls to the search-and-rescue team members.

A few weeks later I got a letter from a lawyer for the county, turning down the reimbursement.

"Perhaps you'd better look for reimbursement from the Trahan family," he wrote, "since it was apparently at their insistence that you appeared here."

There was no acknowledgment that ASAR had been invited into the county by the sheriff, no praise for Dave's work—just this cold letter.

I later learned that the county had its own dog team, and there was resentment over the idea of somebody else coming in with a dog. A union grievance had been filed. Apparently, the sheriff's department was trying to disavow its part in bringing in the people who found Michael Trahan.

The behavior of Dave's dog in the Trahan case was impressive but not surprising. In wilderness searches I had learned that dogs had potential well beyond the things we asked of them in training.

The first time I went on a search alone I took Saki to Troy, New York, to try to find Melanie Palmer, a girl scout who had been missing for a day. On the radio I had heard that State Police Officer Walter Drabble was in charge of the search. I had gone to school with a Walter Drabble and I couldn't imagine that there were two. So I called him up. They put me through to him at the search site, and I told him about ASAR and the dogs.

"I'd like to come up and help," I said.

"With dogs?"

"Yes, with dogs," I said, somewhat annoyed because the police never seemed to take the dogs seriously. "If she's there, my dog will find her."

"Gee, I don't know, Marilyn. We've got a lot of searchers here and . . ."

"You think they'll laugh at the lady and her dog. I know," I said. "Don't worry about it. I can't search until your team has moved out, anyhow. I've got to have the area clear for the dog."

It was six o'clock when I got to the park where the state police and volunteers had been searching all afternoon. The woods were sparse and the land fairly flat. There were few areas that could conceal the girl. The police had concluded that Melanie had wandered away from the park.

"It's all yours," Walter told me. He introduced me to the Alberts, the girl's aunt and uncle, with whom she lived. Walter wished me luck, but it was obvious that the men who were giving up for the night thought this lone lady with her dog was pretty funny.

I asked Walter to take Saki and me to the PLS, the "point last seen." He led me to an open field, the kind of place where families picnic and kids play with Frisbees.

Again he wished me luck. "Did it rain here today?" I called, as he was walking away.

"Yes," he said.

"Not many people in the park?"

"Right," he said. "Why?"

"It means something could have happened to her right here without anybody seeing," I said.

He nodded his head. "I'm afraid so," he said.

I put Saki off lead. He meandered around, probing the air for the current that would carry the scent of a human being if there was one around. The winds were shifting, and though he seemed to alert from time to time, the scent was swept quickly away and he had to search again. His movement came in spurts, but after about ten minutes in the large open field he led me to a man-made pond about fifty feet wide. Much of it was surrounded by brightly painted rocks and it was landscaped with flowers and shrubbery. In the mud near the edge of the pond I could see the shimmering pennies and nickels of people who had made wishes there.

As I followed Saki, I noticed that the rain had slicked down the grass on the edge of the pond. At one point I almost slipped, and I could see that once you lost your footing you could easily end up in the pond, but I didn't give it a lot of thought.

I watched Saki for some sign of alert. He stopped suddenly and I thought he had something. But then he leaped into the water and started paddling across the pond. I was at first disappointed, then intrigued by what the dog was doing. He returned to me after shaking the water from his fur, and we walked around the pond. When we got to the other side, Saki went into a strong alert and again dove into the water. He swam several yards, then turned to me with a praise-seeking look on his face, as if he had done something terribly clever. I noticed that the breeze had shifted direction and that Saki had jumped in at a point exactly opposite the spot where he had leaped in on the other side. And then I knew.

I stood helpless on the edge of the pond, deeply saddened by what I suddenly realized—the girl had drowned—and at the same time terribly impressed by what the dog could do. My god, I thought, a dog can find people underwater. The scent from that little girl had risen to the surface of the water. With an air-scent dog, it had taken me less than an hour to find her. Though I felt empty inside, I gave Saki his praise, just as Al Romeo had taught me, along with a handful of dog biscuits as a reward. I knew that something tragic lay beneath the dark surface of the pond, but all Saki knew was that he had played the game I had taught him so diligently at Utica.

"Good boy, good boy," I said, futilely trying to keep my voice from sounding hollow.

After I told the police what had happened, I took Saki home. The next morning, news reports said divers had found the girl in the pond.

3

In 1972 my mother died. Still in her forties, she succumbed to cancer. For months after her death, I felt as if someone had opened a vein and all my good feelings about life were leaking out. No matter what I did or said, I could not seem to close it up. My mother's death was devastating to me, not just for the tragic loss of her life but for the hard look it caused me to take at my own. What do you want, Marilyn? A family? A career? You don't have forever. Make your choice. Sometimes I thought I could have both. Other times it felt as if I could have neither.

My son, Paul, an adorable redheaded five-year-old by the time my mother died, was crushed by the death of his grandmother. Paul had been as close to my mother and my father as he was to anyone. Many times they had taken care of him when I was working. But they were more than baby-sitters. They played with Paul, they bought him presents, they took him places. After Ma died, Paul became difficult. At times he was a terror. He misbehaved, he threw tantrums, he broke things. In the selfishness of grief I was perhaps not as understanding as I might have been, and I'm sure that I often snapped at Paul when he most needed a hug and reassurance. I often worried about him. He was five, and already he had lost his father and his adored grandmother.

Early in 1973 I became pregnant with my second child. I thought then about giving up search-and-rescue altogether. I didn't see how I could go on rescue missions when so many people needed me. Chip needed me. The new baby would need me. And, perhaps most of all, Paul needed me.

One night before I was to go on a rescue search in the Adirondack Mountains, I stayed up late poring over maps of the region. A young woman, an experienced camper, had hiked into the mountains to draw for two days. After four days she still had not returned. If I hadn't had the search maps to work on, I probably would have found some other reason to burn the midnight oil. Since my mother's death I had been haunted by nightmares, and I could not lie in bed and wait for sleep without becoming frightened. Instead I would stay awake in the living room, working at my desk until I grew so weary that my head fell into my arms.

The night before the scheduled Adirondack search I sat at my desk studying the contours of the search area and trying to pinpoint the high-probability areas. I heard a soft noise coming from the hallway. It sounded like crying.

When I got to the hallway I saw Paul sitting on the bottom stair, dressed in his Donald Duck pajamas, crying his eyes out.

"Paul!" I said. "Why are you crying? What's wrong, honey?"

In the shadows of the hallway I could see that his little head was down almost to his knees. He just shook it back and forth. He had been moody for several days, but this was the first time in weeks that he had actually cried.

"Did you have a nightmare?"

Again he shook his head.

"Then what is it?"

Paul just buried his head deeper and cried louder.

I sat beside him on the stairs and put my arms around him. "Paul, you have to tell me, so I can make it better," I said.

He looked up then, his cheeks red from crying. "I don't want to die," he said. "Like Grandma."

"Oh, Paul," I said. I could feel my heart sink with sadness for him. "Oh, Paul." I pulled him into my arms. "That was different, honey. Grandma was sick. Why would you die?"

"Because there's only one bed," he said. "And when the new baby comes he'll get it and I'll have to die."

Never before had I felt so out of touch with my son's emotions. "My god, is that what you've been thinking?" I asked. "Is that why you've been so sad?" His head, now pressed into my shoulder, nodded up and down.

"Oh, no, honey," I told him. "You're our special child and nobody can ever take your place. The new baby is for all of us."

For a long time Paul and I cried together, and when we were done I carried him up to his bedroom and tucked him in again. I kissed him good night and sat with him for a long time, thinking that I'd better be careful or I would miss some important moments in his life.

In the morning I called Al Romeo and told him I could not go on the search. Later I drove to Albany with Paul and together we picked out a crib for the baby. When we got home I asked him to help me set it up in his room. When it was done we stood together and stared proudly at our work.

"See, Paul," I said, "this is where the baby will sleep. You'll still have your bed."

Paul's behavior improved after that. He was a happier boy, but still the shadows of sadness showed often on his face. The incident on the stairs had taught me that I needed to spend more time with him.

As it turned out, the ASAR team found the young artist who had gotten lost in the Adirondacks. She had been drawing pictures and smoking a lot of pot, so she lost track of time and forgot that people were expecting her home on the third day. When the team found her she was in a clearing, slightly stoned, and dozens of pastel drawings were thumbtacked to the trees that surrounded her.

During my pregnancy I went to all the Utica weekends, except during my ninth month. Chip and Paul even went with me a couple of times in our camper. In December of 1973 the baby was born. We named him Joseph, and I renewed my commitment to being a wife and mother.

Like any new baby, Joey was a handful, so I cut way back on my search-and-rescue activities. I convinced myself that my marriage was improving and that I didn't need something else in my life. But people kept getting lost, and when I was asked to search for them I had a hard time saying no. Often I gave in, and I would pack Saki and my equipment into the camper and drive off, leaving Chip with Paul and the baby.

For more than two years I did my best to keep things in balance. I told myself that as the kids got older I would have more time for searches. I often thought of offering my help.

Each morning, when there was time, I liked to sit in the kitchen and read the paper. Often there were news items about missing people, and whenever I came to one I would find myself reading it two or three times as if it were about people I knew.

One morning in 1976 I sat in the kitchen, slowly turning the pages of the newspaper. I came upon the small headline: "Troy Student Still Missing." I leaned forward and read more intently.

> Where is Kenneth Berry?
>
> This question has puzzled police in Troy, New York, ever since Friday, when the 23-year-old graduate student in electrical engineering was reported missing from his dormitory at college.
>
> According to campus Security and Safety Chief John Ayan, Berry has not been seen by his roommate or anyone else on campus since 8:00 P.M. on Wednesday, when he put on his coat and left his dorm room. Berry took no personal belongings with

> him. None of his family or friends have heard from him for the past week.
>
> Berry, originally from New Jersey, was living in the dorms while earning a master's degree on a full-tuition scholarship from a Massachusetts power company.
>
> He was reported missing by his roommate, Arnold Petrie, after he failed to show up for two days. According to Chief Ayan, a full investigation and search of the campus has turned up nothing.

I put down my coffee and cut the article out of the newspaper. For so long I had been half in and half out of the search-and-rescue field. I had gone to monthly meetings in Utica, but I had stayed away from most searches. Now, as I slipped the news item into the pocket of my robe, I knew that staying away would get harder, not easier.

At noon, when I realized that I couldn't stop thinking about the Berry case, I called the college and asked to speak to Security Chief Ayan. After I told him who I was and offered to help, there was a long silence.

"Mrs. Greene," he finally said, "we could use some help, we really could. This student has been missing for a week now, and I'm not sure what you would be able to do with a dog at this late date."

I explained about the air-scent method and how the dogs didn't track and could be used effectively even after a week.

"There still could be problems," Mr. Ayan said.

"Why?" I asked.

"Well, some people wouldn't understand about the dogs. It could cause credibility problems."

I remained silent.

"Look, I believe in the ability of the dogs. I really do. I've read about some of the things they've done in Europe. But a lot of people here won't look too kindly on a dog on campus. Dogs got a bad image during the civil-rights era. There could be complaints."

I explained that the dogs are not trained for aggression and are trained not to bark on a search. Most are members of their handler's family, living in the house with children.

John Ayan put me in touch with Francis Murphy, the president of the college. Mr. Murphy was also reluctant before he finally approved of my involvement. He said, "So far no one has had any luck in finding a clue of what happened to Ken Berry. His parents have been here every other day. They are very worried. A fresh viewpoint might help."

After I found a baby-sitter for the boys, I called Chip at work and told him I had to go on a search.

The drive to the college took an hour. A light snow was falling. That reminder of the season made me realize that Kenneth Berry must have taken his mid-term exams shortly before he disappeared. I wondered how well he had done.

When I got to the college in Troy a policeman met me at the main entrance. He led me along a twisted path to a row of red-brick dormitory buildings. The policeman was tall and athletic-looking, but beginning to get a bit out of shape. In one hand he carried a Styrofoam cup filled with coffee.

"I can tell you right now, you're not going to find him," the policeman said. "We've looked everywhere twice."

The policeman led me into one of the brick buildings and up a flight of stairs into Ken's room.

He introduced me to Arnold Petrie, Ken's roommate, a tall, studious-looking young man who wore black-rimmed eyeglasses. Arnold had decided to stay on campus at least until Ken was found.

Arnold showed me Kenneth Berry's things. Everything was just as he had left it. His money and other possessions still lay on his desk. Men's toiletries were neatly lined up on his dresser.

"His clothes are all here, too," Arnold said, tugging at

one of those accordion-style closet doors. The clothes, all neatly hung, were expensive and conservative.

"Nothing unusual happened before he left?" I asked.

"No," Arnold said. "Except he gave me his Max Creek tape."

"His what?"

"Max Creek," he said. "It's a musical group we like. They play mostly around Rhode Island and Connecticut. Ken and I went down to see them a few times. It's kind of weird, him giving me the tape."

"Why do you say that?"

"Well, he knows I like them and all, but he could have made a copy. He didn't have to give me his only tape."

"Yes," I said.

Arnold led the police officer and me outside to the parking lot where I had come in. Kenneth's Mustang was still parked where he had left it.

"Did any of his friends have cars?" I asked.

"Ken wasn't very social," Arnold said. "He was kind of a loner."

"How did he do on his mid-terms?"

"I don't know. We don't have marks yet. But I don't think he did as well as he had hoped. Ken had very high standards."

"A good student?"

"Straight *A's*," Arnold said, and I felt a chill go through me. I knew that Kenneth Berry was probably dead.

The fact that he had taken nothing with him, that he had disappeared after taking disappointing exams, that he had given away something valuable, all pointed to a despondent person possibly contemplating suicide. The fact that Ken was a straight-*A* student only increased the likelihood that he had taken his own life. A disproportionate number of suicides by young people are committed by straight-*A* students.

This was just one of a number of patterns that I and other searchers had found among missing people. I had been one of Bill Syrotuck's assistants in his research into the tendencies of missing persons.

He discovered, for example, that small children will be found at a mean distance of 0.3 miles from the PLS and downhill from there, having followed paths of least resistance. Children between the ages of six and twelve will travel a mean distance of 1.6 miles and also go downhill. One curious discovery was that people of any age who are reportedly despondent when last seen, and for whom suicide is a possibility, will be found within 0.25 miles of the PLS and at a higher elevation. Of course, none of these statistical tendencies guarantee a successful search, but they do create high-probability areas, which the experienced searcher eliminates first.

Arnold went back to his dormitory and I led Saki out of the camper and began to search. At the back of the campus, beyond the administrative building, there was a narrow road that led up to a jutting, rocky hill.

"What's up there?" I asked the officer.

"Nothing," he said. "Trees. Kids go up there to drink in the summer. Nobody goes there in the winter."

"I'd better take a look," I said with a sigh.

"What do you think, lady, that we didn't look up there? Of course we did."

"I'm sure you did," I said. "But it won't hurt to look again. You don't have to go with me, if you don't want."

"Believe me, I don't want. But the chief says I have to stick with you."

We set off across the campus. The officer reached down and patted Saki.

"What do you say, pooch?" he asked. "Smell anything yet?"

A cruiser caught up with us about halfway across the campus. It was the officer's partner, a thin, gray-haired man, offering us a ride. The officer got in, and I told him I'd meet him at the bottom of the hill. When I got there, he and the gray-haired man were sitting in the car drinking coffee out of a Thermos bottle. He got out of the car and stared up at the hill.

"You can see all of Troy from up there," he said.

"Do you want me to go ahead while you finish your coffee? It's only a small hill," I said.

"Sure," replied the officer. "I'll meet you on the other side. It's a waste of time, though."

I glanced at the hill again. It was covered with snow and I was sure the footing was bad. Nobody goes there in the winter, I thought. At least, not without good reason. It was a high-probability area. It had to be searched.

The top of the hill was a tangle of bare bushes. Dark and delicate against the wintry afternoon sky, they seemed to be without depth. I sensed that the bushes were hiding something awful even before Saki's ears went back and his body moved straight between two of the larger bushes. I followed behind him. Lost between the bushes, covered by half an inch of powdery white snow, was the body of Kenneth Berry. Inches from one hand was an empty bottle of sleeping pills. Near his feet an empty bottle of vodka glistened under a thin layer of snow. He was here all the time. The search had taken twenty minutes.

Disheartened at the discovery, I walked back to the police car to notify the officials. The officer cranked down the car window just a few inches.

"He's up there," I said.

The officer didn't thank me or anything. "Yeah, okay, okay," he said. "We must have missed him in the snow and all." He called for another car.

I led both officers back up the hill. For a moment the three of us stood out in the cold air, staring down at Kenneth, thinking our own sad thoughts. Then the gray-haired officer turned his back to me and said to the other officer in a low voice that came from between clenched teeth, "Get her out of here."

I felt as if I'd been slapped in the face. Inside, I felt

again like the eighteen-year-old girl who had sat in Walter MacNamara's office and been told there would never be a female state trooper in New York.

I was driven back to my car by one of the officers. Neither of us spoke. Before I got out he surprised me by squeezing my hand. "Look," he said, "you and the dog did good work, but we've been looking for this kid for a week and . . . well, you know."

"Yes, I know," I said.

It took two hours to get home. The snow grew thicker as I got closer, and I stopped several times for coffee, partly to rest my eyes and partly because I was not anxious to face Chip.

I felt heartsick. I had found something I was good at, and yet the people whom I respected treated me as if I had done something wrong. It had happened many times, but somehow I was always taken by surprise.

By the time I got home that night my sadness and disappointment had turned to anger. In fact, I was livid. I paced across the living-room floor, pouring out my story to my husband.

"I was stunned," I told Chip. "Absolutely stunned. 'Get her out of here.' That's what he said. What kind of a thing is that to say?"

Chip was stretched out on the living-room couch. He had been reading a newspaper and now he had politely flattened it against his chest. His eyes were on me, but his thoughts, I suspected, were on the paper.

"Twenty minutes," I said. "That's how long it took us to find that boy. They had no reason or right to talk to me that way."

Chip just looked at me, his eyes shifting back and forth across the room as I paced in one direction and then the other. He didn't say anything. Is he even listening, I wondered.

"Stunned," I said again. "I mean, what had I done

wrong? Only solved a case that had them stymied, that's all. Why did they react that way? I just don't understand it."

"Boy, are you naive," Chip said.

I stopped in my tracks, surprised not so much by what Chip had said as by the fact that he had said anything at all. "Naive, what do you mean, naive?"

"Naive," he said, "that's what I mean."

"Explain, please."

Chip gave me his impatient stare. "Look, Marilyn, to be shown up is one thing. But to be shown up by a woman . . . that's humiliating."

"Humiliating?" I was baffled.

"Yes, humiliating."

"God," I said, "what's the matter, did I bruise their delicate little egos?"

"You're making them look bad," Chip said. It should have been a compliment, but it sounded like criticism.

"I'm making them look bad? They're making themselves look bad," I shot back. "This boy never even left the campus and they couldn't find him. I can't help it if I'm better at this than they are. Besides, the point is supposed to be to find the person, isn't it? Doesn't the victim's family have any rights here? I'm a resource. I'm enhancing their services. Anybody would think they'd be grateful. I didn't take anything away from them. I'd just like a little . . ."

"A little what, Marilyn, what would you like?" Chip sounded as if he were exasperated with me.

"Appreciation," I said. "Is that such an awful thing?"

Chip sat up and tossed the newspaper to the floor. He stared at me as if I were something that had gone sour right before his eyes.

"Appreciation," he chided. "How about appreciation for cooking dinner? How about appreciation for raising your children?"

"It's not the same," I said.

"You know, you don't have to do this," he said. "You do have a family you could take care of."

"I know I have a family," I said. "And I do take care of them." He had struck a nerve. "I don't need you to remind me."

"Okay, forget it," he said. "Look, I work hard all week; I've got my own frustrations. I don't want to spend my evenings listening to you complain about yours. You're beating your head against a wall. Why don't you just give it up? Why don't you just accept reality?"

I think it was in that moment that I understood I really didn't have my marriage and my career, and I never would. I knew that someday I would have to choose between the two.

4

The man had been staring at me for several minutes. We were at a party in Waterford at the home of my friend Fran Poole. Chip was off talking to somebody, and I'd found myself standing alone by the wide glass doors to the garden. It was a lovely spring night. Fran was celebrating a new job, and I had vowed that I would come and socialize and not talk S-and-R shop with her or anybody else. I had just come back from a difficult three-day search in the Adirondacks and it felt good to wear a dress and a little perfume.

The man who was watching me had deep brown eyes and shallow lines etched around his mouth, as if he laughed a lot. He moved toward me.

"Don't I know you?" he asked.

"I don't think so," I replied.

"Friend of Fran's?"

"Yes."

"I'm Roger Spellman," he said, offering his hand.

"Marilyn Greene," I said, shaking it.

"I've been trying to place you," he said. "I'm sure we've met."

For several minutes we talked. Roger told me about his business, plastic something or other. He was quite charming and I felt comfortable under his gaze. Chip and I did not socialize much, so I prized these chances to get out and listen to music and talk about new things. After a few minutes Roger went to the bar to get us each a drink. When he came back, he stopped, handed me the glass, and stared straight into my eyes.

"I know I know you from someplace," he said. "How do you know Fran?"

"Search-and-rescue," I said. "We're both members of Adirondack Search and Rescue."

His eyes widened now and the smile came easily to his face. "That's it," he announced. "I don't actually know you. But I've seen you on television. You're the lady with the dog."

There it was again. The lady with the dog. That's who I had become. I managed a weak smile. I had been hoping that he really did know me or that he was pretending to because he wanted to talk to me.

I didn't really want to talk about it. I wanted to talk about other things for a change.

As my skills had sharpened, my reputation had grown, and I'd gotten a lot of press in the Albany area. Because members of our small search team were scattered all over the state, I went on many searches alone. When I did, I was frequently greeted with open skepticism and looks of disappointment because I was a woman. But when I found a missing person, the story was made more interesting by that fact.

"You do quite a job," Roger Spellman said. "I mean finding people like that."

A few minutes later we were joined by his wife. "Honey, this is Marilyn Greene," he said, "the woman who finds missing people."

He introduced us and soon another of his friends joined us. "This is Marilyn Greene," he told his friend. "Wait till you hear what she does. Tell him, Marilyn."

I felt like I had been placed on stage. Although the missing-person field was important to me, it wasn't what I wanted to talk about at a party. This had happened to me many times before. A few minutes later, when I had drifted away from the small group, I pondered things I could say in the future that would gently change the subject away from my work.

It was an ongoing concern for me, this fear that I was becoming known only for what I did, not for who I was. I particularly remember that evening because later that same night I got a call from a sheriff in West Virginia asking me to bring a search team and air-scent dogs to find a man who was missing in the Allegheny Mountains near the Virginia border.

Although Adirondack Search and Rescue had been formed primarily to search for people missing in the Adirondack Mountain region, our work had become widely known and we often got calls from other states. Typically, I would get a call at three o'clock in the morning, after the state police or volunteers had been searching all day or even for several days. A state-police captain or some other authority would officially invite ASAR to conduct a search. I would then run up an enormous phone bill calling team members all over New York to ask if they could go. Sometimes I would get one other member to go, sometimes four or five. The air force, which has responsibility for all land searches, just as the coast guard is responsible for sea searches, would have an airplane on call to fly us in.

After I ended my conversation with the sheriff that night, I went to my files and pulled out the topographical map of West Virginia, published by the United States Geological Survey. Having a map in front of me was like flying over the area in a helicopter. The maps are highly detailed and marked with symbols, so I could easily find particularly hazardous areas. I found the quadrangle in eastern West Virginia containing the area where the missing person, Herb Meachum, had disappeared. It was rugged, mountainous country. Herb had wandered off a trail, and I could see that on one side of the trail the land rose steeply. If he had gone that way, the difficulty of moving uphill would probably have forced him to change direction and come back to the trail. On the other side the land dropped quickly. Most likely he had drifted that way.

By studying the depressions in the terrain I could see where the land would probably have funneled Herb. In this case an old state highway snaked around the base of the mountain, and I knew that if Herb was uninjured, and just wandering aimlessly, the pull of gravity would bring him to the highway.

The day after the party at Fran Poole's house, the air force flew Fran, myself, and three of the men from our team to Hagerstown, Maryland. From there the state police took us by helicopter into the area where the man had disappeared, a rural and seemingly rugged section of the state. The helicopter pilot objected to having Saki aboard, until I explained that he had been trained to accept aircraft noise and confinement. No pilot would welcome a dog fight while in flight, nor would the team, which is why the dogs received aircraft training.

By this time Saki was fully trained, and I had also taught him not to bark on a search. A barking dog could easily scare a lost child deeper into a hazardous area. And I had taught Saki not to be protective of my car. If I had to send somebody back to the car for emergency medical supplies on a search, any degree of canine vehicle protectiveness would be totally unacceptable.

We made our search base in a small town where there was a police station, a grain store, a church, and a community full of friendly people.

A police officer took me to interview the fellow who had been with the missing man at the point last seen. Fran joined me.

She and I had paired up on this trip. Fran was new to S-and-R and eager to learn.

He was a tall young man with an Adam's apple the size of a golf ball and eyes like big blue glass marbles.

"Yeah," he said, "we was just senging in the woods when Herb disappeared."

"You were singing?" I asked.

"Yeah, senging."

"That's all? You were just standing in the woods, singing?"

"Yes, ma'am, me and Herb go senging in there every year this time."

I looked at Fran. She shook her head.

"Now let me see if I understand this," I said again. "You and your friend were singing in the woods, and he roamed off for some reason?"

"He didn't roam off, ma'am. He was senging and I was senging and we just got separated."

"I see," I said.

Then he looked down and he said, "Goddamn. You ain't got snake boots on. You can't go up there without snake boots."

Fran and I were wearing short hiking boots.

"Snakes?" Fran asked.

"Yes, ma'am," he said proudly, "around here we got more rattlesnakes and copperheads than you can find anywhere in this country."

Fran and I looked at each other, nodded, smiled. We were sure this man was just having fun teasing the gals. Before we gathered to divide up the search area I returned to the state trooper who had escorted us into the area.

"Excuse me," I said, "but I don't quite understand why these two fellows were singing in the woods. Are they part of a band or something?"

The trooper's face lit up and he let out a big laugh. "Not *singing,* ma'am. *Senging.* Senging with an *e.*"

"Senging? What's that?"

"Picking ginseng," he said. "A lot of it grows around here. People pick it and they sell it to some company down in Charleston that ships it to China. The Chinese say it contains the 'elixir of life.' Ain't that something!"

We divided up the search area. Using my altimeter for guidance, Fran and I and Saki worked our way up to about nine hundred feet. In mountainous regions the air currents flow up during the day and down at night. So we searched the whole area at nine hundred feet and then moved down to the next level and searched. I had learned always to search back and forth, never up and down. That can be a killer. I checked the altimeter from time to time, because a searcher, as much as a missing person, will tend to drift downhill.

Most of the area was thickly wooded and the going was slow. Saki was often distracted by small scurrying woods animals.

At one point Fran and I stopped to rest the dog. I sat down and leaned against a shady sycamore tree. Who are we kidding? I thought. We're resting ourselves, not the dog. I pushed my head back and let my eyes go out of focus. I liked the way the sunlight was sprinkled between the trees, making lovely patterns of light and dark that shimmered like the surface of a pond as the branches above me swayed ever so slightly in the breeze. The greens and browns of the forest were soothing colors. I took a deep breath, wishing, as I sometimes did, that I could move to an enchanted forest and live in a tree house.

Then a gust of wind rushed through, pushing the branches around, and the light shifted in such a way that I suddenly realized the patterns of light had camouflaged snakes. Dozens of them. Fran and I were surrounded by snakes. Snakes as long as my legs were curling around trees, sliding over fallen leaves, and slithering around stones.

"Fran, I think we'd better move on," I said. "Don't ask me why."

After that, we moved more quickly through the snake-infested, ginseng-producing woods that now seemed not quite so enchanted. Late in the afternoon we came upon an old shack set in a clearing in the woods. It was a comical-looking place, sloping and sagging at all sorts of angles, as though it had been picked up, carried ten feet, and then dropped. A stream of smoke rose through a round tin chimney poking out of the tar-paper roof.

From the looks of the place, it must have been home to a large family. Half-a-dozen small children came up to us, some of them dragging broken bicycles behind them. A skinny woman who looked undernourished stood silently by the side of the house.

There was one man on the porch sitting in a cushioned rocking chair. He seemed to be the patriarch of the family. He looked seventy. He was probably fifty. I asked him if he had seen any sign of this fellow Herb.

"Yeah," he said.

"Do you know where he is?"

"No, but I could find him."

"Where would you look?"

"Don't know," he said.

It took me a few seconds to translate each of these replies because the man was fiercely chomping away at something.

"Is that chewing tobacco?" Fran asked. I don't know why she asked, except that she's curious about everything.

The man on the porch smiled as if Fran had asked to see snapshots of his kids.

"Yeah," he said and he pulled this disgusting wet blob out of his mouth. "See," he said, "you chaw it on the one side till the spit is white, then you chaw it on the other till the spit gets white. Dentist says it's good for you."

This man didn't have a tooth in his head.

The man mercifully returned his chewing tobacco to his mouth, and Fran and I moved on.

When we got in that night, still Herbless, the sheriff was waiting to take us to our motel. Sometimes on a search we'd sleep in a school or other donated quarters, and sometimes a local motel would donate rooms to the search team. We told the sheriff about the snakes and he got very concerned. "Oh, yes, ma'am. This particular area is famous for having more snakes than anyplace in the country, and we got the rodent population to support them. I'm surprised nobody told you."

The sheriff was a fat, easygoing sort of man, quick with a joke and polite as could be.

"Say, would you ladies mind if we made one little stop before I drop you off?" he asked. "I want to show you something. You being from New York and all, I want you to get a look at our new jail."

To him New York meant the big time, even though to us it meant places like Schenectady and Syracuse.

He drove us into town and pulled up in front of a low red-brick and cement building. It was the brand-new police station and county jail. The section of seeded soil in front was marked off with string and posted with a big sign that said: "Don't even think of walking here. Grass growing."

The new building, simple though it was, looked almost futuristic against the background of the older southern homes that lined the narrow street in the center of town.

The sheriff showed us his new office, then took us downstairs to the jail and introduced us to his prisoners as if they were family. "This is so-and-so," he would say, leading us along the three new cells on either side of a concrete corridor, "he murdered so-and-so—and sitting over there, that fellow with the guitar, that's Clem Mason, shot his daddy last Saturday, yes, ma'am."

After we were done visiting, the sheriff drove us to the Hickory Motel, where the ASAR team was staying. Somehow when Fran and I got out of his car with our gear and the dog we also managed to walk off with the sheriff's flashlight, maps, subpoenas, and a pad of blank traffic tickets. He would go crazy all the next day looking for them while we were in the woods looking for Herb and avoiding poisonous snakes.

After we were settled in our room that night, there was

a knock on the door. It was Richard Dennis, a member of our search team. Richard looked worried.

"What's the matter?" I asked.

Richard, who had almost no sense of smell, said, "I think maybe my dog got near a skunk today. Would you mind coming in and letting me know?"

I left Saki in our room while Fran and I followed Richard to his room, which he was sharing with Al Romeo, who had run for the hills. When Fran and I got to the room, Richard had his German shepherd at a stand-stay and he was running his nose over the dog's fur to see if he could detect the odor of skunk. To him there was a faint odor. In fact, the stink was overwhelming.

"Christ, Richard," Fran shrieked, and we backed out of the room, holding our noses.

When we got back to our room we found that Saki had lain down next to a table with a rickety leg. The leg had come off and the table had tipped, spilling a lamp and knocking a mirror to the floor.

So by the time we had been in West Virginia twenty-four hours, the ASAR team had racked up quite a score. We had destroyed a motel lamp and mirror; walked off with the sheriff's flashlight, maps, and subpoenas; and left one motel room embedded with the smell of skunk that probably lingers to this day.

If the West Virginia trip was more lighthearted than most, it was perhaps because all of us sensed on our arrival that nothing tragic had happened to Herb. After all, these were his hills.

As it turned out, we were right. Late on our second day of searching, one of the local searchers finally went into the valley near the highway. Normally you don't search near a highway for an adult whom you believe is alive. If a person is near enough to hear the traffic, then he's not lost.

The searcher came down to a ledge along a dirt road that rose along the hill next to the main highway. When he sat down to take a cool drink from his canteen, a skinny young fellow came along and sat down beside him. The two men started talking. The searcher told the fellow about the search for a missing man, and the skinny fellow told the searcher about how he'd been out senging for a while. Then the fellow got up to leave.

"How long you been out here?" the searcher asked.

"'bout five days," the man said.

"Five days! What's your name?"

"Herb."

"Herb? You're the fellow we've been looking for. Why didn't you tell me you were lost?"

"I ain't lost," Herb said. "I'm right here."

Apparently, he was in the habit of wandering off for several days at a time, and it never occurred to him that people would think he was lost.

Unfortunately, I had learned from experience that the occasions when missing people return alive from the wilderness, either on their own or with a rescuer, are rare. Overall, ninety-five percent of missing people do turn up alive; but in wilderness searches, which is what ASAR was all about, many of the victims are dead. Whenever I would search a high-hazard area more than a week after a person had disappeared, I would be fairly certain that the subject had not survived.

Of course there were exceptions. We all knew of people who had survived in the wilderness for several weeks. Those were the cases that insulated us from total despair. But the dedicated searcher knows better than anyone that the odds are never good. You study the area. You look at a map. You ask how the weather has been lately. You learn about the missing person's physical condition. You count the days that have gone by. And all of this accumulated information usually leads you to an unwelcome, but inevitable, conclusion. The missing person is probably dead.

As my skills at finding people in the wilderness increased, so did the weight of my heart, because my efforts rarely saved a life. Certainly I was bringing to families at least the comfort of having an answer to the disappearance and a release of some of the emotional strain. But it was still rarely a happy ending.

For a long time I tried to look beyond the fact that lives were not being saved. I was a professional brought in to solve a disappearance and I would pour all of my skills into solving the particular case: What happened? Where did he go? Why couldn't he find his way out? How could I look at a map and define some high-probability areas? This for me was the challenge, and I could only hope that as searching techniques became more widely known, they would be utilized sooner and then lives would be saved.

But I knew that I was working much too closely to people who were in pain. Pain which is that severe radiates, and it invades everyone who comes close to it. I was feeling it, but I didn't always know that I was feeling it.

Most of the people who are lost in a wilderness area, and do not survive, die for two basic reasons. First, lost people may tend to panic and overextend themselves physically, and in doing so fail to take safety measures, such as building a shelter. And, second, in many parts of the country, search-and-rescue teams that are highly skilled and a valuable resource are used only as a last resort.

Typically, the first people in a search area are the authorities, who in many instances do not have any special training in searching or search management. If a healthy child or an influential citizen is missing, a search party may be formed, but the group may be made up of untrained volunteers. If the missing person is an elderly person, an autistic child, or someone with Alzheimer's disease, the police search may be little more than perfunctory. "Couldn't find anything," I've heard many times, and then the search is terminated. Would a fire department work half a day trying to put out a fire and then leave because they haven't put it out? I don't think so. What rankles me even more is that when the authorities depart, generally they offer no advice or information to the family.

In the summer of 1976 I went to Vermont to look for a twenty-year-old autistic man who, ten days earlier, had wandered away from a private school near the village of East Corinth. The sister of James Loubier, principal of the school, had seen my name in the newspaper and called me for help. After a long day and night of searching, with Loubier by my side every step of the way, we sat in a meadow at sunrise, knowing the man may not have survived. Loubier was a small, trim man who still wore the suit, vest, and necktie that he had worn on the previous evening when I had met him. Through a long night of searching he had not unbuttoned the vest or loosened the tie. I sensed that it would not seem proper to him. He told me that his wife had died and that the school had been his whole life. He had always been haunted by the fear of a tragedy like this. When it was my turn to talk, I told him about search-and-rescue teams, about the air-scent dogs, about help from the air force and the civil air patrol, about all the things that could be done to find a missing person within hours of his disappearance. And this man just looked at me, tears in his eyes, and asked, "Why didn't the police tell me about this?"

I had no answer for him. The subject of the search was found dead the next day.

As the years of searching went by, the sadness and the frustration built up—but through it all I had the necessary fire. Despite the traveling, the inconvenience, the family friction, the expense of being a volunteer, and the many tragic discoveries in places so beautiful you would think no one could die there, one overriding fact kept me going. People were disappearing and we weren't finding them fast enough.

It meant the world to me to be good at something, to have some purpose in life. And if there were times when I bristled at the idea of always being identified by strangers as "the lady with the dog" or "the lady who finds dead people in the woods," I had to remind myself of those desperate days early in my marriage to Chip when I felt as if I had no identity at all.

Although I had learned an enormous amount from Bill Syrotuck, it also seemed to me and others that I had a natural talent for finding people. More and more I just seemed to go to the right place, which only enhanced the feelings of frustration over not being called in when the search was two hours old instead of two weeks old.

I became intimately knowledgeable with the tools of my job. The map, the compass, and the altimeter never felt foreign to me. I have a good sense of where a lost person would go, and a sense of direction that has never failed me, day or night.

Once I went into the woods near Hartford, New York, late at night with Guido Pitteli, a Syracuse businessman whose son had been missing for ten days. When the days were hot, I preferred to search at night. It was easier on me and easier on the dogs. Mr. Pitteli, who had accepted the fact that his son was dead, was skeptical about the search.

"At night?" he asked.

"Yes. It doesn't make any difference when you're working with dogs."

"But won't we get lost?"

"No. North is still north, south is still south. The hills and streams are still in the same place."

After we had been searching in every possible direction for four hours in the dark, I could hear the man's anxiety. It was understandable, of course. He had lost a son to these woods.

"You're sure you can find the way out of here?" he asked softly.

"Actually, we're going to come out on the road exactly where we went in."

When I led him out of the woods I was disappointed to

find that I had brought him out a hundred yards from where we had parked the car. I had expected a better performance from myself. But then he looked at the car and he looked at me and he said, "I can't believe it. Right on the money."

Well, Marilyn, I thought, if that's good enough for him, it ought to be good enough for you.

It was two days later that I found his son's body. Fortunately, I was alone. He had broken a leg. I think he had climbed a tree and fallen out of it.

As I learned to use the tools of my unpaid profession, I learned also to balance my family's needs with my own. Chip and I had come to an uneasy truce over my search-and-rescue activities. In addition to being a housewife and mother, I worked at various jobs outside the home, so I felt entitled to leave him with the children and the chores from time to time.

Although Paul had been jealous of Joey at first, as older siblings usually are, my two boys got along well together. I still worried about Paul. I wondered what damage, if any, had been done to him by the loss of his father and grandmother. Often Paul was moody and often he was mischievous, but the good times convinced me that my worries were unwarranted and that both boys were headed for healthy adolescence.

A husband and two boys were not the only family members I had to worry about. As Saki grew older, I knew that I would need one or two years to train a new dog for searches, so I got a German shepherd puppy and named her Kili. From time to time, Chip let off steam about the epidemic of dog hairs and the fifty dollars a month I was spending on dog food, but for the most part he was good-humored about the canine invasion. Saki and Kili were great with the kids, and I would have wanted them as pets even if they didn't have such special talents.

Everything was in balance, though delicately so. As time

went by, my frustration over always being called in too late had the effect of broadening my interest in missing-person cases. I wanted to learn more about all the categories of missing persons: the runaways, the parental abductions, and the throwaways—children who had been abandoned by their parents.

There was a much greater scope to the missing-person field than simply people lost in wilderness areas. I had a desire to expand my knowledge beyond what I had now.

5

"You want me to do what?" Paul asked incredulously. His eyes twinkled, and he tried to hold back a smile. We had played this game many times before.

"Climb a tree and stay there," I said. This was the autumn of 1977. Paul was nine and I had taken him to a wooded area about three miles from the house. It was a conservation district where there wouldn't be other people around to confuse Kili.

"That's it?" he asked. "Just climb a tree and stay there?" He shook his head as if he couldn't believe that anybody would ask such a thing. By this time Paul had helped me train dogs dozens of times, but he liked to put up a fuss each time I asked and act as if his mother were weird for wanting him to climb a tree and stay there. It was a running gag with us.

"Well, how long do I have to stay there?" he asked.

I smiled. "Until Kili finds you."

"What am I supposed to do up there?"

"Here," I said. I gave him a stack of new comic books as a bribe. His eyes widened. "Okay, Mom, for you I'll make this sacrifice." He looked around. "Which tree do you want me to climb?"

"Any one," I said. "I don't want to know which one. I'm going to drive Kili about half a mile down the road and then we'll cut back into the woods. Don't make any noise, okay?"

"What if I break my leg climbing the tree, can I scream?"

"No," I said.

Paul and I spent that day together, much of it chasing each other through the woods and bombarding each other with motley piles of fallen leaves.

"Got you," I would say, and Paul would run off giggling, screaming behind him. "You didn't get nothing, Ma. Not a single leaf touched me." And then he would come charging at me with his pile, throwing it so hard that he would lose his balance and fall over.

Of course we were there to train the new dog, too, and five or six times that day Paul climbed up a tree to read his comic books and wait. Whenever Kili found him, boy and dog would be equally excited. Kili would plant herself at the bottom of the tree where Paul was hiding and she would wait for me. Paul, up in the tree, would send her bouquets of "good girl, good girl," and when he got down we would give Kili a stick to retrieve as her reward. I would compliment Paul, too, on his choice of tree, his quiet, his patience. Paul, as much as Kili, seemed to get from these forays a much-needed sense of accomplishment. He took pride in his ability to stay still and quiet in the tree while the dog sniffed the air for a scent of him. I knew how important it was to be good at something, and for a while I had high hopes that Paul would get as enthusiastic about search-and-rescue as I was. He really was enthusiastic for a while, but there wasn't much he could do for me besides hide in trees; and as my family's resentment over the time I devoted to search-and-rescue seemed to move inexorably toward an explosion, Paul's enthusiasm seemed to wane.

In November, Joey, anxious to be part of "Mommy's work," was too young to be climbing trees. But when we woke one morning to an early and fairly heavy snow, I gave him his chance. I wanted to train Kili in snow. If a person is buried under snow, his scent will rise through it to the surface, which is why in Europe the air-scent dogs had been a primary avalanche search tool for years.

I bundled little Joey up as warmly as I could and I took him out to the same wooded area where I had gone with Paul. I left Kili in the car and I buried Joey in the snow, so that Kili could search for him.

I had Joey all buried, with just a small opening for his nose and mouth. "You okay, pal?" I asked.

"Fine, Mom," he said. He giggled. Joey thought being buried in snow was a riot.

Then I heard footsteps crunching in the snow behind me.

"Hold it right there, ma'am," a deep male voice said.

I turned around and saw a New York State trooper. His car was pulled over on the highway, right behind mine.

"Oh, hello," I said.

"Do you mind telling me what's going on here?"

Joey didn't make a sound.

"Huh? Oh, I'm burying my son in the snow," I said, knowing how it looked.

"I see," he said. "Any special reason?" He glanced suspiciously at the pile of snow.

"I'm training my dog to find him."

"I see," the trooper said. He walked to the snow pile and crouched down so that his face was right next to Joey's.

"You okay, son?" he asked.

Joey's eyes were closed and he said nothing.

The trooper glanced at me, as if he expected me to start running.

"Are you okay, son?" he asked again.

Joey still said nothing, though I knew he couldn't hold the smirk on his face much longer.

"Joey, will you tell the officer you're fine—or they're going to put your mother in jail," I said.

Then came the giggles, great waves of them, and Joey, heaving with laughter, shook off all the snow I had so carefully placed on him.

The officer stood up.

"The boy seems to be okay," he said, and he left.

There were moments of great fun with the kids, all the more precious because they involved the sharing of my love for search-and-rescue work. The feelings of joy that I experienced in those moments seemed to grow more intense that fall—perhaps because I sensed that they would soon come to an end.

Two nights before Thanksgiving the phone rang at ten o'clock. Paul and I were sitting in the living room playing cards. Joey was sleeping.

"Is this Marilyn Greene?" the voice on the phone asked. Static crackled across the line and I knew it was long distance. I also knew I was about to lose Thanksgiving with my family.

The call was from a colonel with the Air Force Rescue and Recovery Service (AFRRS). He told me that a man by the name of Mason Heiden had been missing for three days in the wilderness of Hayward, Wisconsin.

"We realize that tomorrow is the day before Thanksgiving, ma'am, but the situation is pretty desperate," the colonel said. "We were wondering if you could go out there with a team. They had a pretty heavy snowfall the night Mr. Heiden disappeared, so there's nothing to track. We thought maybe you could do something with your air-scent dogs. Heard there's only seventeen of them in the country. That right?"

"I'm afraid so," I said.

I told the colonel I would come, and he promised to put a plane on alert in Albany.

I hung up the phone, feeling angry with myself for agreeing to go but knowing I would be angrier with myself if I had said no.

"Sorry, Paul, I have to go."

It didn't require explaining. By now I had made almost a hundred search-and-rescue trips.

Paul made a face. "Oh, Ma!"

"I know, I know. But a man is missing. He could die if I don't go."

"So let him die."

"Paul!"

"What about Thanksgiving?" Paul said. "What about dinner? How are we going to have a turkey if you're not here?"

"I'll try to get back," I said.

"You'll try?"

"Yes, I'll try. A man's life is more important. When you're grown up you will have hard decisions to make too."

After I listened to Paul's feet stomping up the stairs and his shutting the door, I took a deep breath and started making phone calls. I knew that getting a team together would be hard. By 1977 things had changed. Bill Syrotuck had died. Several members had dropped out of ASAR. Morale was low. Mine was, too.

But I didn't want to go to Wisconsin alone. I was tired of explaining that, yes, I am a woman and, yes, I do search for missing people and, yes, I do find people and, no, I don't think it's a job best left to men. It was easier just to let a man get off the plane ahead of me so I wouldn't have to deal with all that. Besides, I wanted at least one of my own people at base camp.

Late that night I lay awake in bed beside Chip, working on the dialogue I would need. I hadn't yet told him. It had always seemed to me that there must be a way to get across to Chip the importance of what I was doing. After all, these little trips were not shopping sprees; they were matters of life and death. My presence could make the difference for a lost person. And yet, whenever it came time to tell Chip that I was leaving, my words always sounded weak, even to me. This night was no better.

"I'm leaving for Wisconsin in the morning," I said. "There's a man missing."

Even as I spoke the words it was clear to me that Chip already knew I was going somewhere. My silence, my tenseness, my whole demeanor gave me away.

"Just do whatever you want," Chip said coldly. "I don't want to hear about it." He rolled over. His words and the silence that followed stung me as I lay awake through most of the night.

Early the next morning the team flew to Wisconsin in a C–130, a big, rumbling, slow-moving four-prop plane. When we got over Hayward in northwest Wisconsin, near Lake Superior, it looked as if we had been diverted to the North Pole. I stared down at a desolate area of ice and snow, now and then pierced by areas of pine forest, which looked from the air like islands on a white ocean. As we moved in close to our destination I snapped on the earphones so that I could listen to the pilots.

"Looks like the landing strip is all ice," I heard one say through a crackle of static. "Have to reverse the engine, can't use the brakes."

Then the other: "Looks to me like the strip is not even big enough to put this thing down."

Oh great, I thought, I'm going to give up Thanksgiving with the family, and we're going to end up landing in Boise, Idaho, or someplace.

"Well," I heard, "from the looks of the tracks, something pretty big has landed there. Let's go for it."

I felt the plane begin to drop. Down went this big dragon of a plane into the white wilderness, aiming for some icy little airfield that neither of these guys had ever been to before. We hit the surface with a thump and the plane started fishtailing left and right, skidding on the ice. The engines reversed and the plane began to slow down and finally slid to a stop. Okay, I thought, they got it in. But are they going to be able to get it out? From my window I could see what must have been obvious to the pilots just before they touched down: The tracks that had looked so big were made by a truck, not an airplane.

Bill Vought was the first one off the plane, followed by Bob MacKenzie, then Sue Suchoff and myself.

A deputy from the sheriff's department was there to escort us to base camp. He rushed over to Bill and pumped his hand enthusiastically. "Thanks for coming," he said, and he introduced himself. Then he glanced at Sue and me and said, "I see you brought your own cooks."

"Well, no," Bill said somewhat sheepishly. "Actually, I'm the cook. This is Marilyn Greene. She's the search coordinator."

"You don't say?" the deputy said, and that was the last we heard from him for a while.

Base camp is headquarters for a search. It can be a police or fire station, but usually it's a clearing within the search area. It is there that a base operator stands by with a walkie-talkie, medical supplies, a stretcher, food, and whatever else a victim might need in a hurry. At base camp the search is coordinated so that several searchers do not cover the same area; and when a searcher radios in that he has found the victim, the base-camp operator arranges for helicopters, sleds, or whatever help must be sent in to get the victim out.

Base camp is also where the exhausted searcher goes to recharge himself with food and rest. When we got to the base camp at Hayward there were a lot of weary men in blizzard suits drinking coffee and trying to keep warm by a campfire. The deputy walked over and spoke to an old forest ranger, who I gathered had been in charge of the search. I followed. When I got to the ranger I smiled and extended my hand to him.

But his hand didn't come back to meet mine. He stood there glaring at me. I listened to the sounds of a chopper in the distance. The cold and the sense of isolation absorbed me. I would have welcomed a smile. Instead the ranger's face turned red with anger. He pointed a finger at me, and he started poking my chest just below the throat, pushing me backwards.

"Look here, young lady," he bellowed, "I've been a ranger many years. I've been up three days' straight now pushing these crews to find this man, and I don't need anyone coming in and upsetting the apple cart."

He pushed me once for every word, as if he were punctuating his words. Pretty soon we were backed up to the campfire, where a large pot of hunter's stew was cooking. Everyone had stopped talking. They're watching us, I thought, and I felt as if I were on a stage and didn't know my lines. I hadn't done anything. I hadn't even said a word. Damn, I thought, I haven't even introduced myself. And here was this angry man poking at my collarbone like an arrogant bully. Suddenly I was fed up, not just with this guy but with all the insulting people I had ever dealt with.

"Listen," I said, "are you under the impression that I have come here to replace you?"

"You're damn right," he said, with his hands on his hips.

"Well, you're wrong," I shouted. I wanted to slug him. Instead, I shoved my fingers into his chest and started poking him as hard as he had poked me, pushing him back in the other direction.

"You're wrong," I said again. I had a lot of wrongs to purge from my system and when I had poked him as far back as he had pushed me, I turned abruptly and walked away, vowing that I would never again let somebody push me around like that.

The deputy followed me and apologized for the ranger's poor manners. But I was in no mood for apologies. The helicopter had settled down at base camp.

"Is that chopper for me?" I asked.

"Yes, ma'am."

"Well, I came here to conduct a search," I said, "so let's

get on with it." I was still seething. Leaving the rest of my search team to work at base camp, I climbed into the chopper with the deputy and the ranger and Saki, who settled in quickly and plopped his head on my lap. Saki was getting as comfortable with airplanes and helicopters as he was with the living-room couch at home. As the helicopter lifted us into the sky, which had dumped its snow and now had turned a startling icy blue, the deputy told me about the missing man.

Mason Heiden was a wealthy sixty-six-year-old real-estate manager from the Milwaukee area. He had gone hunting with his two grown sons. Still hampered by a childhood leg injury, he had gotten too weak to go on. The sons had left him at a deer stand while they hunted. When they got back, their father was gone.

As we flew over the area I could see that I didn't have as many miles to worry about as I had thought. Most of the trees below me were hardwoods. They were young because the area had been lumbered out, and at this time of the year they were too bare to hide anything. I could even see rabbits scampering across the snow. If there were a man down there, I would spot him from the helicopter.

But there were three areas where a man would be difficult to see. They were small, triangular clusters of conifer trees, dense little forests that concealed the ground beneath them. I poked at the windshield of the copter, pointing out the dark areas.

"He's in one of those," I said to the deputy.

"No, ma'am, we already searched those areas."

"Not with Saki, you didn't," I said. "He's there."

The helicopter landed at the spot where Mr. Heiden had abandoned his rifle and his knapsack. Several searchers were already there, along with patrolmen from the town of Hayward and Robert Heiden, the missing man's son.

"This is where he dropped his rifle?" I asked a police officer.

"Yes."

"He'll probably be found within one-and-a-quarter miles of here," I said.

"Oh, Jesus!" I heard the ranger say. "A psychic. They sent me a goddamn psychic."

Maintaining a calm professional tone, I said, "When a man abandons his rifle and his knapsack he's in a very desperate situation. He is almost always found within a mile and a quarter of that spot. When you know about probabilities like that, you know where to look first."

I knew I was preaching at the man, but I was still angry.

All three of the coniferous triangles were within a mile and a quarter of that spot, so I didn't rule out any of them. I was sure that Mr. Heiden was in one of them. I was also sure that he was dead.

I climbed into the back seat of a pickup truck where Mr. Heiden's son Robert was sitting, staring grimly out as if he might spot his father on the horizon. He offered me coffee from a Thermos bottle.

"I really appreciate your coming," he said. "I mean, with Thanksgiving and all."

He was in his mid-thirties, a handsome, healthy fellow who looked as if he hadn't slept for a while.

"What do you think happened to your father?" I asked. I was trying to feel him out. I wanted to tap into his emotions to see if he understood how bleak the situation looked. The abandoned rifle, the snowstorm, the harsh surroundings, the elapsed time, and the missing man's age and injury, all left little room for hope.

Robert Heiden looked me in the eye, searching my face to see if there was any hope there. Then he reached across the seat of the truck and gently touched my knee.

"Look," he said, "I'm a doctor. I understand that my father..." The words caught in his throat and he turned away for a moment. He looked at me again. "I understand... about my father," he said. "But this is not right." He waved an arm as if to indicate the miles of flat, cold land that surrounded us. "This is not a Christian burial."

I placed a hand on his shoulder. "That much I can give you," I said.

"Thank you," he said.

I took my dog and left. One of the Hayward patrolmen, Robert Cammack, asked if he could come with me. I supposed these men figured that if a rich hunter could get lost out there, it could happen to a lady with a dog. They were just trying to protect me, I guess, so I told Cammack to come along. I was calming down now, and Officer Cammack was very personable.

We searched all afternoon, first in one of the heavily wooded areas and then in the second. When we left the second, I was certain that Heiden was in the last of them.

By the time we got to the third triangle, the light had seeped out of the sharp blue sky and the shapes of the trees were beginning to merge with the darkness. In late November, Wisconsin gets dark pretty early. We worked by flashlight.

After we had been pushing our way through the swamp brush for ten minutes, Saki went on a strong alert.

"He's here somewhere," I said.

Saki started moving faster, and we had to work hard to keep up with him. "Good boy, Saki," I kept calling. "Good boy. Go find him. Good boy."

For a long time we followed Saki through the tough underbrush and the stiff crusted snow. Finally, after we had been following him for half an hour, Saki stopped dead in his tracks and refused to move. We had come into a circle of tall trees that might look inviting to a person desperate for protection.

"He's here," I said, remembering that same sense of certainty I had felt about Kenneth Berry when I had climbed the hill in Troy.

Officer Cammack and I swept our flashlights across the

darkness. Nothing. Again we covered the area with our lights. Still nothing.

"He's not here," Officer Cammack said.

"Yes, he is," I said.

It took several more passes with our lights to find Mason Heiden. He was under some pines and was half covered with snow. It appeared he hadn't made it through the first night when it rained, just before the temperature dropped. He would have been hard to discern even in daylight. It was possible that searchers had walked right by him.

"God," the officer said, "what a shame." He pulled out his walkie-talkie and prepared to speak into it.

"No," I said.

Officer Cammack stopped and looked at me.

"I'll call in," I said, somewhat sorry that I had startled him.

"Sure," he said. "Whatever you want."

I knew that the man's family was at base camp, and I didn't want to repeat a bad experience I'd once had when I found a young girl who had drowned. The policeman who was with me then had gotten on the radio and said, "We found the girl's body." I can only imagine what that sounded like to the parents who were waiting near the radio at the other end. I didn't want the Heidens to learn of their father's death by overhearing it on a walkie-talkie.

"Base camp, this is Unit 7," I radioed in. "I am with Unit 27."

"Unit 27" let the base-camp operator know the victim was dead. If I had found Heiden alive and well, I would have said I was with Unit 22. If he were alive but in need of medical assistance, it would be Unit 23.

Bill Vought was on the base-camp radio.

"Unit 7, do I read you correctly? Did you say you are with Unit 27?"

"Yes," I confirmed. "Unit 27."

Patrolman Cammack and I sat for five hours in the cold darkness of that woods waiting for more men to get through with a sled to take the body out. I had given them my compass bearings, but Cammack had to fire his gun in the air several times to keep them coming toward us. They had to hack away much of the underbrush with machetes to make a swath wide enough for the sled. When they got there, the police photographer's camera wouldn't work, so I used my Roliflex to take the evidence photos for them.

When we returned to base camp it was after midnight. The hunter's stew was still cooking over the campfire. The coroner was there. He was a comical older man who walked over to me, leaned in close, and in the conspiratorial tones of a fellow professional asked, "Ma'am, what do you suppose Mr. Heiden died of?"

"Hypothermia," I whispered.

"Hypothermia, huh?" he said. He smiled and his tone told me he didn't know the meaning of the word. But he walked confidently over to his assistant, who asked him the cause of death.

"Hypothermia," the old man replied with great authority.

Light moments at grim times, I thought, wishing there were more of them.

Robert Heiden's face was weary. He hadn't slept much since his father's disappearance, but in his eyes I could see some sense of relief. At least it was over.

"Dad will have a proper burial now," he said. He took off his gloves and rubbed his hands together against the cold, then offered me a hand to shake. "We'll know where he is. It means a lot."

For a moment he seemed unable to leave, as if there were more to say but he didn't know what it was.

I spoke. "Sometimes I get frustrated because I'm called in too late, and I know that I could have found somebody alive if I'd gotten there sooner," I said. "This wasn't one of those times."

"I know," he said, and he walked slowly back to the truck that would bring his father home.

Sue, Bill, and Bob had put in long hours at base camp and we were exhausted as we headed back to the motel in Hayward. We slept until eleven the next morning. It was Thanksgiving. When we walked downstairs, everybody who had been involved with the search was there. They had brought turkeys and all the trimmings. They knew we had given up Thanksgiving with our families. We all had Thanksgiving dinner together, and I enjoyed every bite despite occasional pangs of guilt whenever I wondered what my children were having for dinner.

My heart was heavy as the C–130 flew me home to Albany. I thought a lot about Mason Heiden and all the other people who had died alone. It saddened me. When I got home, the mood in my house was a lot colder than the Wisconsin woods had been. I had left my family at Thanksgiving and they were angry.

Chip spoke to me. What he said was, "Three hundred dollars, Marilyn! Three hundred dollars. I've been doing some figuring, and that's how much you've spent on this damn search-and-rescue foolishness just in the past month."

He was sitting at the kitchen table writing out checks for the monthly bills. There was even a message in that, since I usually took care of the bills.

"I'm sorry," I said.

"You're sorry. Great. Well, we can't eat *sorry* for Thanksgiving dinner or any other meal. These people are taking advantage of you, can't you even see that? What you do is valuable and you're not getting a penny for it. You're not even breaking even. You're spending money. Our money."

"Well, I'm not doing this to make money," I said.

"That's for damn sure," Chip said. "Why are you doing it?"

"Because it's what I do."

"Because it's what you do? What is that, some kind of pop-psychology bullshit? What does that mean? Why do you do it, Marilyn? Just tell me, why do you do it?"

"Because I can hear them crying," I said. I hadn't thought to say it. It just came out.

"Who?" Chip's tone softened suddenly. He could see that I was close to tears. "What do you mean?"

"I don't know exactly," I said. "It just came to me. A memory I hadn't thought of in years just flashed in my mind."

I pulled a chair away from the table and sat down. I was shocked by the unexpected memory and the realization that I had blocked it out for twenty years. I lay my hand on the table. Chip gently placed his hand over mine.

"When I was a kid in Burbank I had a little friend named Donny," I said. "I hadn't thought of him until just this moment when you asked me that question. One day I was walking down the street where Donny lived. As I approached his house I heard yelling. His parents were having a fight. And then I heard a gunshot and Donny came running out of the house toward the sidewalk. He was screaming, 'He's killing my mother! He's killing my mother! Somebody please do something! Somebody help!'

"There was no one there; just me. I just stood there. I was twelve years old.

"Donny's mother came running out of the house toward me. She was screaming. Then Donny's father appeared at the door with a gun in his hand. He leveled it at Donny's mother and I jumped as I heard the shot. Donny's mother stumbled when the bullet hit her in the leg, but she didn't fall, she kept on going. Donny's father fired the gun again an instant later, and the second bullet went through her arm. It spun her around and then he fired again. I saw the bullet go through her neck and she fell to the ground. Then the man went back inside the door and I heard another shot. Young as I was, I knew that he had committed suicide.

"Neighbors came outside and I'm sure the police were already on their way. Donny stood there on the lawn near his mother. He was crying in a way that is hard to describe. No words. His hands were outstretched and he was crying right out. He had such a look of terror, grief, and helplessness. I didn't know what to do. A neighbor put an arm around Donny and it was as if the neighbor weren't even there. Then the man picked Donny up and took him away. Donny didn't look back, he just kept on crying right out in horror."

As I told Chip this, I could feel the tears well up in my eyes. His hands were holding mine. It seemed as if years had gone by since I'd felt such gentleness from another person.

I took a moment to compose myself. The sudden memory had upset me.

"The thing that comes back to me the most clearly is the way Donny cried," I said. "I'll never forget it as long as I live."

Chip held my hand even tighter. I was sad for Donny and for myself and for the connection that had been lost between my husband and me. I was also sad for the moments I hadn't spent with my children.

I looked at Chip. "When I search for a missing person, that person's family is crying in the same way," I said. "Maybe you can't hear it, it's still inside of them, but it's there. And I don't want to stand there helplessly ever again."

"Look, honey," Chip said, "I understand how you feel, I really do. But this hobby of yours is just not working out for this family. You can see that, can't you?"

"Yes," I said.

"When are you going to give this up? We can't afford it."

"Right now," I said.

"Huh?"

"I'm giving up search-and-rescue. I'm tired. Nobody cares about it except me. It makes you and the children unhappy. I'll quit."

"Good," Chip said. "I'm glad to see you come to your senses. It will be nice to see an end to the insanity around here."

6

"Marilyn Greene?" asked the voice on the phone.

"Yes," I said. I glanced at my watch. I was late for work.

"My son has disappeared," a woman said. "Officer Mullaley said I should call you. He said you can find people."

"Tony Mullaley?" I asked.

"Yes. He told me you found Sarah Rand."

Tony Mullaley was a state trooper. He was one of the few who knew quite a bit about air-scent dogs. We had been on several searches together, and our relationship was a good one.

This was December of 1978, and for a year I had more or less kept my promise to quit searching for missing people. I had gone on only a few searches, when I just couldn't bring myself to say no. The most satisfying of them had been the search for Sarah Rand, because I'd helped to find her alive, and I never left the house to do it. Sarah was an elderly woman who was suffering from Alzheimer's disease. She had wandered away from a nursing home in western Massachusetts. By studying maps of the area I had been able to determine the high-probability area where she was later found. I did it by telephone. When they found Sarah exactly where I'd said she would be, she was happily picking wildflowers.

"Look, I'm not sure if I can help you," I said to the woman on the phone. "Tell me about your boy."

It hadn't been twenty-four hours since my most recent decision to positively, absolutely give up looking for missing people, and already my emotions were being turned by a distressed woman on the phone.

The woman's name was Sue Vale, and her fifteen-year-old son, Gary, had vanished ten days earlier.

"Gary went to school the same as usual," she told me. "He took his books with him and he said that he was going bowling after school. He just never came home."

"Have you reported him missing to the police and did they conduct a search?" I asked.

"Yes, the police know he is missing. They found out he did go bowling after school but no one has seen him since then. They searched the woods but now they say he ran away. I know my son, Mrs. Greene. He didn't run away. Will you please help me find him?"

God, I thought, don't these people know what this does to me? I was torn between my decision to quit and my desire to help this woman. With two boys of my own, I could imagine how she must feel having a son missing for ten days.

For what seemed like several minutes I held the phone in my hand and just stared. "I'm on my way to work right now. Can I call you from there in an hour?"

"Okay. But, please, help me," she said. "I don't know who else to turn to."

I told myself that I hadn't made a decision yet, but on the way out of the house I pulled a New York map from my file cabinet and stuffed it into my pocketbook.

By 1978 both my boys were enrolled in school, and I had taken a job as a program analyst for a nearby municipality. My job was to implement programs for housing projects. It was a job that could have been rewarding but wasn't, because I spent most of my time on the bureaucratic treadmill, and it seemed as if everything got talked to death and nothing meaningful ever got done.

When I got to the office, all of my fellow workers were in a meeting, which is where everybody usually was. I didn't wait. I went straight to my desk and called Mrs. Vale.

"Okay," I said, "I'll do what I can." I spread the New York map across my desk. "Tell me where you are."

The Vales lived in upstate New York in a tiny town on the Vermont border. I asked Mrs. Vale where her house was and where the bowling alley was. I could see immediately that the wooded area between the bowling alley and Gary's house was a giant circle. The two points were almost exactly opposite each other on that circle. If Gary had tried to take the shortest route home, he would walk through the woods and his path would take him close to a slate quarry. I told Mrs. Vale I would be there the next day.

It took three hours to drive to the Vales' house. Mr. and Mrs. Vale were both there waiting for me. She was a slim woman with very long red hair. He was short, bearded. He was an engineer, he said, but he hadn't been to work since Gary disappeared. They both looked scared. As we sat in the kitchen, drinking coffee, Mr. and Mrs. Vale took turns describing to me the last day that Gary had been home. They described each moment in such detail, it was as if they were handing me snapshots of their son.

"Gary would never run away," Mr. Vale said, just as his wife had said on the phone.

"Yes, that's right," Mrs. Vale said. "He just isn't that kind of kid. We had small problems, sure, but nothing major."

"But nobody just disappears," Mr. Vale said.

Although they kept saying that Gary would never run away, I thought they were hoping I would convince them otherwise. When a teenager is missing, the parents need to believe that their child might have run away, no matter how painful that might be. It's the least-frightening possibility. If a kid has been missing for ten days and hasn't run away or been abducted by a parent, then the situation could be more serious. I didn't say that to the Vales, but I'm sure they knew it.

I asked to see Gary's room. I wanted to know exactly who Gary Vale was. What kind of a kid was he? What, if anything, was bothering him? What did he dream of doing, where did he dream of going?

Gary's room, on the second floor of this small country house, was a typical teenaged boy's room. The bed had been made, but all the clutter of clothes and record-album jackets and half-finished science projects had been left alone. Posters of Ron Guidry and Bill Walton decorated the wall behind Gary's bed. And on the other walls there were posters of hot-air balloons.

"What about other cases?" Mrs. Vale asked. "I mean, when a kid is missing for ten days, what does it usually mean?" There was an edge to her voice, as if she were on the verge of a breakdown.

"It usually means he's run away," I said. "And the parents always think their child wouldn't do such a thing, but believe me, your child can keep a lot of feelings from you."

As I spoke I was thinking about Paul, who seemed more and more to be keeping his feelings locked inside.

From the window in Gary Vale's room I could look down into the Vales' backyard. A huge oak tree towered over the house, and very high on the tree someone had constructed a plywood platform. A series of boards had been nailed to the trunk of the tree as a ladder.

"What is that?"

"Oh, Gary made that," his mother said. "He likes to sit up there, especially in the spring."

"What does he do?"

"Oh, he just sits there with his feet dangling, and he reads. Sometimes he just kind of meditates. You know how teenagers are. Lots of important thoughts."

"I see," I said, thinking that this is a boy who doesn't have the normal fear of heights.

I spent another hour with the Vales, asking them about Gary's girlfriends, hobbies, places he wanted to go, the possibility of drug use, anything that might help me think about where Gary had gone. It gradually dawned on me that I was not approaching this disappearance as I would a wilderness search. I wasn't sticking to the maps and the dog and the PLS. Instead, I was probing into the nature of the person who was gone. What was there in Gary's life that would make him disappear? Was it his interest in science? Was it sports? A girl? Was it his love of high places? Was it some secret about him that nobody else knew?

Before I left the house that day, Gary's father took my hand.

"We really appreciate your helping us like this," he said. "Maybe this can help pay for gas or something." He filled my hand with a fifty-dollar bill, which I later donated to ASAR. It was the first time I'd been given money for searching.

I couldn't get any of the ASAR people to join me in my search for Gary Vale. Terribly discouraged by always being talked into cases too late to save a life, many of them had given in to the pressures of normal family life and turned away from search-and-rescue activities, just as I had. When they heard that Gary had been missing for ten days, they were sure that this was another body search, and they all declined.

So I called Seventy-six Search and Rescue, a Guilderland, New York, group which had been formed in 1976. Seventy-six Search and Rescue had been started by a group of rock climbers, and many members of the team were experienced in high-angle searching. The group, which did not use dogs, was very good at grid searches and rock work.

Early the next morning we moved into the wooded area between Gary's home and the bowling alley where he had last been seen. I took Kili into the woods on the other side of the highway. It was still virgin woods, with a lot of birch trees and tall oaks like the one in Gary's yard, but here and there a section had been plowed away and I could see that a housing development was only a year or two off. While I searched the woods, the volunteers from 76–SAR worked around the edges of the slate quarry. There was a truck road which wound down into the quarry, but much of the perimeter was just a precipice that dropped off suddenly and went down for about two hundred feet to a bottom of water. Sharp ledges protruded like shelves from the walls of the quarry, all of which had to be checked.

Whenever a high-hazard area exists near the place of a disappearance, it is sound practice to search that area thoroughly so it can be eliminated from consideration.

It was a bright, cold afternoon, and some of the rescue workers built a fire in a barrel near the edge of one of the cliffs. We returned to it often to report in and warm our hands. We searched all day. Kili never went on alert and the Seventy-six Search and Rescue crew went up and down the sheer walls of the quarry without seeing a sign of Gary. I was getting hopeful that we wouldn't find him there. If we did, he almost certainly would be dead. If we didn't, then there was the possibility that he had run away and he was alive and well. Pressing down on me as I worked my way through the woods was a share of the fear that I knew Mr. and Mrs. Vale were feeling.

Just before dark, Gary was found on one of the ledges. One of the Seventy-six group called me on the two-way radio.

"Down there," he said, when I reached the edge of the quarry. The light was going fast from the sky and I had to stare hard to see where he was pointing. About a hundred feet from the top and a hundred feet from the bottom, a broad dark ledge jutted out. I squinted, and as my eyes adjusted to the grainy colors of stone I saw Gary Vale. At the top of the quarry were his books, probably sitting just as he had left them. I suspected that Gary had been sitting fearlessly on the top on a large slab of rock, much as he had sat on the platform in the oak tree in his yard, and probably the rock had given way beneath him.

"Was he a friend of yours or something?" a fireman asked. I knew that for the first time on a search I was crying. I was weary and I wanted to go home. But I couldn't, not yet.

Dark descended quickly and the quarry seemed to grow deeper as the sun set and the lights from the parked fire trucks lit the wall. We edged along a thin ledge to the spot where Gary was. A Seventy-six rock climber had set up a safety rope along the route for us to use. A couple of volunteer firemen came with us. We stood nearby while a police photographer worked at the scene. By now Gary's parents had been told and they stood at the top of the cliff, holding each other in grief.

When the police were finished examining the scene, it was the job of the volunteer fire company to bring Gary out. The Seventy-six rock climbers remained to provide whatever assistance might be needed.

"Oh, that's disgusting," one of the firemen said when he saw Gary's body. "I'm not touching him." Another young fireman giggled. I understood that this was the laughter of the fearful, and that we are all occasionally guilty of it. People who are really that callous wouldn't volunteer their time to a fire department. But now wasn't the time for silent understanding. I knew how easily a voice can travel along the wall of a quarry and that the people at the top could probably hear this conversation. I turned the man around by his arm and said, just loud enough for him to hear me, "You think it's disgusting? Let me tell you something, there are people up there who love this boy more than anything in the world. People who would give anything just to be able to hug him one more time. They think he's a beautiful boy, who's gone forever. So why don't you just shut up."

Nobody said much after that, and late that night I thanked the searchers, then I went home and phoned Tony Mullaley, the state trooper who had given my name to the Vales.

It was about ten o'clock in the evening, so I apologized

for calling late but explained that I felt he would want to know that the search was a success and Gary Vale had been found.

There were moments of silence on the phone, then Trooper Mullaley said, "Oh, how embarrassing." He hung up on me. I never heard from him again.

I later learned that the authorities had referred the Vales to me in an effort to take some pressure off themselves. I wasn't supposed to find him. They just wanted to be able to say that they had tried everything.

The next day I moped around all morning. By midafternoon I was disgusted with myself. Marilyn, I said, this is ridiculous, you're acting like a jerk. Go out. Do something for yourself. So I did. I went to Friendly's Ice Cream at the Colonie Shopping Center for a large marshmallow-fudge ice-cream cone with chocolate sprinkles on it.

After I got my cone I strolled out to the mall and sat on a bench near a fountain. As I admired the plants and the little waterfall, I tried to center myself into a more peaceful state of mind. It was just a week before Christmas and the mall was busy. I didn't want to be with people, I didn't want to talk to anybody, but I did want to be in a busy setting and hear voices around me. I wanted to feel plugged into humanity. My eye was drawn by a small, slender old man standing about twenty feet away from me. Smartly dressed and silver-haired, he sported a tan that made him look as if he'd just gotten off a plane from Florida. He caught me looking at him and began to stroll in my direction. I thought of leaving. I just wasn't up to having a conversation. But I was still listless and sad, and I didn't have the strength even to walk away.

When he got close to me I could see from the cut of his clothes and the jewelry he wore that he was well off.

"Young lady," he said, "I'm going to tell you the secret of success."

Oh, god, I thought, why me?

"Yes," he said, sitting down beside me on the bench just

as if I had invited him. "The secret of success is you pick a subject, any subject, and you learn everything you can about it. Not for one year or two, but for ten or twenty years, and you will be a success. Me, I chose real estate. I can walk down any street in America and I can tell you what each house will be worth ten years from now. My wife, Dorothy, she learned about antiques. She can pick up an object at a garage sale and tell you how old it is, what it was used for, who manufactured it, and how much it should cost. Dorothy knows antiques. So remember, pick a subject, any subject, become an expert at it, and you will be a success."

I don't remember if this old fellow said much more. He had said enough. Something clicked. When he left he patted me on the shoulder, and it was as if he wasn't a person at all but an image that had floated into my life just long enough to deliver an important message, and then floated out again like George Burns in the movie *Oh, God.* For a long time I sat there thinking about what he had said, and I realized that I had already taken his advice a long time ago.

I had learned about missing people. I had studied hard and worked even harder, and I was really good at finding them. Damn it, Marilyn, you are good, I told myself. I went over and over it in my mind. What had I done? Who had I found? What did I know? Marilyn, I thought, you're an expert. And in my heart I knew I didn't want to give up the thing I was good at, the thing I loved doing most of all. I wanted to make it my life's work. It was at that moment, with the help of that mysterious old man, that I decided to make my profession finding missing people.

7

She was a short woman, slight and dark-haired, with large eyes that seemed to convey a sense of innocence. Her name was Roberta Garlandi, and it was said that she had found many missing people through the use of psychic powers. Had she? Had anybody? That's what I wanted to know, and so I had called her up, and she had invited me to visit. I had driven six hours to her small ranch house in Pennsylvania.

She was waiting at the door as I pulled into the driveway. "Come in, come in, dear. I could feel you coming," she explained. I walked in behind her, wondering if I had spent years reading maps, training dogs, and trekking through the wilderness to accomplish something that this woman could easily do through some inexplicable psychic power. Half-a-dozen calico cats shared the house with her, and astrological symbols were painted on the walls. The smell of strawberry incense filled the air.

Roberta was warm and gracious. We sat down in her kitchen while Roberta warned me about an "age of difficulty" that would soon vex mankind.

I told her I had become a professional searcher for missing people and was looking for qualified resources for clients, as well as knowledge of any successful people in the field.

Instead of jumping into complicated cases right away, I had concentrated on educating myself. I read articles about the techniques investigators used to solve cases. I learned to use the tools of my trade and compiled a list of people who might be a valuable resource in the future.

For years I had been curious about psychics. "Is she a psychic?" was often the first question people asked when they found out what I do. It seemed as if most people believed in psychics. I wasn't sure. I really wanted to know if there were people with extrasensory powers who could find missing people or assist me on cases.

"Is it true?" I asked Roberta. "Have you really found people?"

"Oh, yes, dear, hundreds of them," she replied. "Let me show you."

She dashed into another room and came back with a long black jeweler's tray. Neatly arranged against the velvety black surface were awards given to her by various police departments.

"For solving crimes," she explained. "You see, dear," she said, "I don't have powers. The powers work through me. I get tens of thousands of letters from all over the world. I wish I could answer them all."

I asked her to tell me how she did it, but she could not. "I just know," she said. "I just know."

I spent two hours with Roberta Garlandi. She offered to do a reading for me, based on nothing more than holding a piece of my jewelry. I slipped off my wedding ring. She held it in her hand and closed her eyes.

"Oh, dear, I'm so sorry about the trouble in your marriage," she said. And then, "But there will be a new man in your life."

Not likely, I thought.

After that Roberta got into specifics of my life, the number of children I had, a problem with one of my tires; and she gave me the warning that I would lose my pocketbook within the next couple of days unless I was careful. None of her information was on the mark, and after a while I found myself trying to help her. When she said that I was troubled by pains in my neck I told her that she was right, even though the pain I had been experiencing lately was really in my lower back, probably from hunching over while I read the books on investigation techniques that I'd been borrowing from the library.

By the time I left I was as uncertain about psychics as I had been when I got there. At one point in our conversation Roberta said that she had worked on a case near Albany, along with a state trooper named Jake Pierce. I knew Pierce very well. We had been on several searches together.

"Oh, yes," Roberta said, "they loved me up there. I found a lot of people for them."

I decided that I would call Pierce when I got home.

I telephoned him late that night.

"Jake," I said, "I talked to a friend of yours today. Roberta Garlandi, the psychic."

There was a long pause and then Pierce said, "Oh, Christ. I hope she's not around here."

"Roberta says she helped you solve some cases."

"Marilyn," he said, "the woman is cracked. She ought to be certified. We were working our asses off, trying to find where some savage had put the three women he had killed. He had admitted to burying them in a swamp. He took us to it. So we're up to our knees in swamp water for about a week, and this psychic Garlandi lady comes along uninvited. She stands out on a dirt road and goes into a trance, twitching her fingers and moaning, 'Oh, they are here. My children are beckoning to me, they are here.' 'No shit, lady,' I said, 'we've only been digging around in this swamp for a week.' Marilyn, this woman's trance is the weirdest thing you ever want to see."

A few months later Roberta Garlandi called to tell me about a disappearance that she was working on. A wealthy couple, Gerald and Lillian Spenser, had been driving through Louisiana on their way to Houston, Texas, when they vanished.

"The Spenser children have hired me to find their parents," Roberta said. And then, after a long sigh: "Marilyn,

I've been down there, but I'm just not getting much. I'm going again next week. I've arranged a fee for you. I thought perhaps you could come down and approach it from a different angle."

I smiled. Somehow common sense, logic, and legwork had become "a different angle."

"I get water," Roberta said, "I get water. That's all." She explained that she wanted to go into a psychic trance and describe places. My job would be to find those places. It wasn't my idea of the best way to search, but I knew I could do some looking around on my own, so I said okay.

When I hung up the phone I said to Chip, "I'm going to take a couple of days off from work and go to Louisiana on a case."

"Jesus, Marilyn!" he said.

"I'm getting paid for it," I said proudly. This would be my first paid job as an investigator.

"Oh," Chip said. "That's different."

I flew down to Louisiana with Saki and drove to a small town near the state line, where I met Roberta along with the Spensers' grown son and daughter. The son, David, was the optimistic one, though he seemed almost nervously so. Not yet thirty, he was bald across the middle of his head, with only tightly coiled tufts of brown hair clinging to the sides. When he spoke he constantly waved his right hand, which almost always held a cigarette.

He told me that for thirty years his parents had been partners in business as well as in life. Starting with a small music shop in the early 1950s, they had built a chain of sixteen music-and-record stores. In all that time they had never had a honeymoon. "We could never even get them to take a few days' vacation," David said.

The trip in their new Mercedes was to be the long-awaited honeymoon. They were driving west through Louisiana to Houston to visit friends whom they hadn't seen for many years.

A few miles short of the Texas state line they checked

into the Manor Motel. They dressed for dinner and then left. On the way out, Mr. Spenser, known by his friends as a great joke-teller, shared a few stories with the desk clerk. Then the Spensers asked the desk clerk about a restaurant called The Chuck Wagon. The clerk recommended it. They told him they would eat there. Late the next day the desk clerk went to their room to remind them of checkout time. Their clothes were there, but they were not. They never came back.

"I'm not real concerned," David said. "I mean, I'm concerned, but I'm not worried, if you know what I mean. They just took off someplace on a whim. You know, the young honeymooners and all that. Did I tell you what a joker my dad is?"

The daughter, Kate, short and apple-cheeked like her brother, was more direct about her apprehensions.

"Mrs. Greene," she said, "I'm really afraid that something terrible has happened to my parents. You hear so many things these days. I'm not sure about this psychic stuff, but we had to try something."

Roberta had already gone into a trance. Instead of describing places, she was telling the Spenser children that their parents would be found on July 10, which was about three months away. I couldn't help wondering, what was the point of my searching for the Spensers if they weren't going to be found for three months. But there was a good chance that Roberta was wrong, so I decided to search.

It was an oppressively hot April day, and as Saki had gotten older he had gotten less and less fond of the heat, so I waited until after dark. I took Saki into the woods near the Manor Motel. I didn't think the Spensers had gotten lost in the woods, since their car was missing, too. But there was always the chance that they had been abducted and taken there by someone who stole their car.

After we had been on a narrow dirt road for about half an hour, Saki and I came to a narrow river. The only way to cross it was to walk over a bridge that looked like a series of six-inch-wide pipes spaced at odd intervals and various heights. It was the strangest-looking bridge I had ever seen. Saki took one look at that bridge, with its wide gaps between stepping places, and decided "no way." He wouldn't cross it. At first I wasn't too keen about crossing it either, but a weak side rail gave me something to hold onto for balance, so I gave it a try.

Leaving Saki behind, I gingerly made my way in the dark across the bizarre-looking bridge, aiming the beam of my flashlight ahead of me. When I got to the other side I came to a stand of pine trees and then a clearing. There was only a fraction of a moon and the pine trees that towered over the area made the clearing darker. I stood quietly. It was one of those odd moments when your life catches up with your thoughts and you can feel that sense of being alive, totally in the present, not regretting, not dreaming, just being. I spent the moment being aware only of myself and thinking what an odd profession it was that had led me into the Louisiana woods alone at night, with a dog waiting on the other side of a weird bridge. Suddenly the moment ended. Something didn't feel right. There was a presence near me.

My skin began to feel just the smallest bit tighter around me. I lifted my head up. I kept still. I thought I heard something move. I scanned the field with my flashlight. I didn't see anything. Again I scanned with the light. This time I swept my light very slowly across the darkness in a long arc. I remembered the lights in Ticonderoga sweeping across a mountain in search of three children. What was my light searching for, I wondered. As I reached the end of the arc something flashed at me. It was a pair of eyes watching me in the dark. A very big pair of eyes. I turned the light back to the spot that had flashed at me. There, staring at me, was a full-grown lion.

The lion stood up and stretched.

I kept myself calm as I started backing toward the bridge. Saki was waiting for me on the other side, and once I crossed back over we ran for the car. It wasn't until I got back into my motel room that I came to the full realization of what could have happened if I hadn't scanned the area first with my flashlight.

The next morning while briefing the local sheriff I told him what had happened.

"Golly, ma'am," he said. He spoke with a deep southern accent. "I sure meant to tell you about that. That's Bill Walton's island you were on. Bill collects wildlife. He buys lions, monkeys, and whatnot from zoos that are closing or those that don't want the animals anymore."

"Aren't you concerned," I asked, "about having a lion roaming around loose?"

The sheriff just laughed. "Naw, Bill's got himself an animal-proof bridge. You see, ma'am, a lion won't even put his paws on a bridge like that on account of the gaps. Only a human can walk on a bridge like that. And, anyway, there are warning signs posted completely around the island. You probably didn't see them in the dark, but they're there."

I spent the rest of the day searching the woods on the safe side of the bridge. Roberta had decided to spend the day in her room, "getting in touch." David and Kate Spenser had gone to Houston to try to get some more investigators on the case. That night I stayed awake for hours in the dark of my motel room, going over the case in my mind. The police thought that somebody must have robbed the couple, killed them, and hidden their car. But I disagreed. The car hadn't shown up. The credit cards hadn't been used. And none of Mrs. Spenser's jewelry had surfaced. More and more I was sure that this was an accidental disappearance.

I went to The Chuck Wagon, the restaurant where the Spensers had planned to eat. I talked to the night hostess, a woman my own age who, as it turned out, had once lived in New York. She allowed me to pore through the credit-card receipts for March 26, the night of the disappearance, something the police had already done with no luck. I was hoping that the Spensers had charged a meal at The Chuck Wagon and that the police had overlooked the receipt. If I could verify that the Spensers had, in fact, eaten at The Chuck Wagon, it would be a lot easier to determine a search area.

"No luck," I said, sitting at the hostess's desk during the dead hours before dinner time. I had gone through the receipts four times. "I suppose there's no point in checking the reservation list, since the Spensers asked about the restaurant on their way out of the motel," I said. But then it occurred to me that I should never overlook anything. "But can I see it anyhow? The reservation list for March 26."

"We don't take reservations," the hostess said.

"Oh."

"Just the waiting list."

"Huh?"

"We just keep a list of people who are waiting for a table," she said.

"You mean, if the restaurant was busy that night, their names would be on a waiting list?"

"Sure."

"What happens to the lists?"

"Probably in the storeroom," she said. She took me to a small closet next to the rest rooms, where old restaurant records were piled helter-skelter on several wobbly wooden shelves. She blew away some dust on an upper shelf and brought down half-a-dozen hardbound notebooks. "That's March," she said, handing one to me.

I opened the book to March 26 and there it was. "Spenser," misspelled, but with a "2" next to it. I was sure it was them. They had eaten at The Chuck Wagon.

As I drove back to the Manor Motel I eyed the road carefully. I counted bridges, and I saw that to return from the restaurant to their motel the Spensers would have had to drive over six bodies of water, six possible water concealment sites. When I got back to the motel I called the weather bureau to find out what the weather had been the night of the disappearance. I was told that there had been a torrential thunderstorm that night. Knowing how slippery a heavy rain can make a southern highway, I felt there was a possibility the Spensers had gone into the water somewhere.

The next morning I walked over every bridge that they would have crossed. When I got over the deepest water on the longest bridge I found what I was looking for. In the six-inch concrete barrier that marked the edge of the bridge there was a tire mark that went up to a ragged cavity where a chunk of concrete had been ripped out, indicating that a car or something had gone over.

Someday I'll need diving equipment, I thought. Too many searches led to water. But all I could do then was to go with my best guess. I was sure that Mr. and Mrs. Spenser were in that water. I took photos of the bridge.

I was due to fly home that afternoon, and the Spenser children were still in Houston. I put the photos in an envelope and left it for David and Kate at the front desk of the motel, along with a letter detailing my suspicions and suggesting that they send a diver down to look. Then Saki and I went home.

A week later I was at home cooking supper for Paul and Joey when the phone rang.

"Hello."

"Is this Marilyn Greene?" an angry male voice asked.

"Yes."

"Well, who do you think you are, telling the Spensers that their parents drove off a bridge? These people are none of your business. Why are you writing to these people?"

He was hysterical, and he hadn't yet told me his name.

"Who is this?" I asked.

"Curt Martin."

I recognized the name. Curt Martin, a Pennsylvania police officer who specialized in missing-persons cases, was a friend of Roberta Garlandi.

"I was hired by the Spensers to find their parents," he shouted.

"So was I!" I said.

"Well, who do you think you are?" he asked angrily. "This is none of your business. What do you know about finding missing people?"

"Quite a bit," I said.

"Oh, really. Have you ever found anybody?"

"Yes."

"But, have you ever really found anybody? I mean really found a missing person?"

"Yes, I have," I said.

He was still enraged.

"But have you ever actually put your hands on a missing person?"

"Yes, as a matter of fact, I have," I said.

Now he was beside himself. "Do you have a private-investigator's license?" he hollered.

For a long time I was silent. He had been wrong about everything so far; I hated to spoil his record.

"Well, no," I admitted.

"Well, miss, for your information, you can be reported for doing this without a private-investigator's license. Just who do you think you are?"

I hung up the phone, feeling uneasy. I knew I would have to apply for a license, but I wasn't sure I could get one. My career seemed to be in trouble before it had really begun.

A few days later, David Spenser called. He thanked me for my work and told me that he and his sister had decided not to have someone search the water. I didn't pry into his reasons. I imagine he and his sister preferred to believe that their parents were still alive, and they did not want to be confronted with what the divers might find. The Spensers never were found, and the water has never been searched to this day.

A week later I was still angry about my phone call from Curt Martin. I knew I would have to get a license before I could accept another case, or Martin would somehow find out about it and possibly cause me legal problems.

On Thursday afternoon I took a deep breath and called the New York State Secretary of State's office and told them I wanted to apply for a private-investigator's license. They gave me an appointment for the following week to see Dale Freeman, whose job it was to screen all the people who wanted to be private investigators.

"Tell me what you've done," Dale Freeman said. He was a soft-spoken young man, blond, with a Boston accent. We sat in his downtown office, and for twenty minutes he listened patiently while I told him about my years of experience in finding missing people. About halfway through the narrative, a big redheaded man, whom I gathered was Freeman's superior, came in. Freeman introduced him as Mr. Butler. Butler sat down across from me and listened to my story without comment.

"Okay," Freeman said when I finished. He tapped a pencil on his desk top. "Let me explain to you that we have a problem here. What you've done is very impressive. But the state of New York requires that before you can even apply for a private-investigator's license you must have at least three years' experience as a police officer above the rank of sergeant, or three years' experience working for another private investigator."

He dropped his pencil and stared into his hands. I could see that he didn't like telling me this.

"Let me see if I understand this," I said, somewhat tensely. "You're telling me that I can't be a private investigator because I was never a police officer?"

"Essentially, yes."

"And I've told you that I couldn't even apply to be a police officer because of the restrictions placed on females."

"Yes, I know how things used to be."

"So aren't you really saying that I can't be a private investigator because I'm a woman?"

"Well, I wouldn't couch it exactly that way," Dale Freeman said, "but I guess I can see your point."

"But what about all the searches I've been on? I can show you dozens of letters of appreciation I've gotten from police departments all over the country."

"But you didn't get paid," he said.

"Excuse me?"

"You didn't get paid for searching."

"Well, no. I did it as a volunteer."

"Then it's not professional experience," he said. He shook his head. "Not if you didn't get paid," he added.

"You're telling me that I'm being penalized for donating my time to people who needed help?"

"I know it sounds unfair," he said, "but that's the rule. If it's volunteer experience, it doesn't count."

"But I've been called in by the FBI, the state police, and the United States Air Force," I said.

He shook his head. "But it's not professional experience," he said again, perhaps hoping it would make sense this time. "You didn't get paid for it."

"This is incredible," I said.

Mr. Butler had listened to all of this without comment. Now he spoke up. "Dale, can I speak to you in private for a minute?" he asked. The two men walked out of the room.

I sat alone in the office trying to comprehend exactly what this rejection meant to me. I could go on search-and-rescue missions, but I couldn't have a professional career finding missing people. I could look for people, but I couldn't charge for my services. By this time the

New York State Police had begun accepting women, and I could probably get in. But my heart wasn't in it. I was stuck.

When Dale Freeman came back into the room he was alone. He sat down again at his desk and smiled.

"Mrs. Greene," he said, "I don't want to get your hopes up, because I know this is important to you. But I've just been discussing your case with Mr. Butler. He's the division head here. Now, there is a passage in the law that says 'or other qualifying experience.' I don't know whether the secretary of state will look upon your background as qualifying experience, but I can give you the proper forms."

"Then I can apply for a license?"

"Not exactly," he said. He rifled through a row of file folders in his desk and pulled out a long white form, which he slid across the desk to me. "All this form does is allow you to *apply* for an application. Then if you are granted the right to apply, you will receive an application, and if that is accepted, you will have to take a test."

"I can apply to apply, is that right?" I asked.

"Yes."

We both smiled at that. It was as if we both knew we were in a mental ward called state government.

"But, look," he said. "Send it back to me and I'll send it along with my recommendation that you be allowed to apply. I think you'd be . . ." He paused.

"What?"

"What I'm trying to say, I guess, is that the field is not exactly crowded with upstanding citizens right now. I think you'd be a credit to the profession."

As it turned out, my timing had been perfect, although I didn't know it. State civil-service regulations had prohibited hirings or promotions based on work experience that was voluntary. If you hadn't gotten paid for it, it didn't count. A group of women had filed a lawsuit saying that this was sexual discrimination, since women did most of the volunteer work. I had walked into Dale Freeman's office at a time when this was on everybody's mind, and I suspect that the word "lawsuit" had come up in the discussion with Mr. Butler while both men were in the other room.

The next day I filled out the form which allowed me to apply to apply. Then I waited.

A month later I came home from work one night and an envelope from the New York Secretary of State's office was the only thing in the mailbox that wasn't addressed to "resident."

I carried the envelope into the house and placed it on the kitchen table. The house was empty. Paul was off playing and Joey was with the sitter. I was alone—just me and the envelope, which had suddenly become the biggest thing in the room, and I was afraid to open it.

I poured myself a cup of coffee and I pulled a small butter knife out of a kitchen drawer. Then I sat down at the table and stared at the envelope.

Would they let me in or not? Did the past ten years count for something? Did my experience have value? That's how I saw it. The state of New York was about to pass judgment on me, and my future was about to be announced. I had no alternative. If I couldn't work as an investigator, I didn't know what I would do with the rest of my life.

Finally, I told myself that the envelope didn't know anything about me. It couldn't contain a judgment of who I was. It could only contain someone's decision about what I would be allowed to do. I slipped the butter knife under the flap and opened the envelope, and with trembling hands I pulled out the papers. I unfolded the first one. It was a letter from Dale Freeman.

"Dear Marilyn," it began, "Congratulations." I read the rest of the letter with a broad smile and through eyes that were wet with tears.

8

I couldn't figure out who would send me a dozen red roses, but they stood in a vase on the dining-room table when I got home from work. They lit up the room. "For Marilyn" the little envelope said. I picked it up and ran my fingers across it a few times, trying to guess who had sent flowers.

I knew what the occasion was. My private-investigator's license had arrived in the previous day's mail. It had been three weeks since I'd taken the test. The questions had not been difficult. They also had nothing to do with being a private investigator. The questions were things like, "A food-service worker at a state penitentiary should count the kitchen utensils after every meal because: (a) it's important for all state employees to save the state's money; (b) you don't want metal utensils in the hands of dangerous criminals; (c) it's important to have the same number of knives, forks, and spoons."

Who would send me flowers? Perhaps one of our friends, although there weren't many to choose from. Chip and I led a very quiet social life. I had Fran, he had Gizzo, and we had just a few couples over for dinner now and then. At another time the roses might have come from my father, but by this time he was quite ill with cancer, and he had been depressed for so long, ever since my mother died, that this sort of gesture was just no longer in him. I could imagine Paul and Joey sending me roses, but I knew there was no way they could have gotten the money, and they certainly wouldn't have addressed them to "Marilyn."

I tore open the envelope and read the card.

"Congratulations, honey, on getting your private-investigator's license. You worked hard for it, you deserve it. Chip."

For a moment I stared at the roses and then at the card again. I put it down, feeling pretty dejected for a woman who had just gotten a dozen roses. They were lovely. The gesture was lovely. But my own husband had sent them and he was the only person who hadn't occurred to me. How sad, I thought.

As touched as I was by the flowers, I knew that they didn't change anything. Chip and I had long ago gone from being husband and wife to being just friends. We knew that our marriage was dying and that the end was not far off. And perhaps at some level we sensed that my investigator's license was as symbolic of its ending as the marriage license was of its beginning. In fact, I had already brought up the possibility of moving out. With my father sick, and my license in hand, I was feeling more and more the need to be back in the city.

"Do what you think is best," Chip had said, without rancor. "Whatever you think is best."

A few days after the roses came I drove to my housing-authority job. But when I pulled into the parking lot I just sat in my car looking at the front door of the building. I could not bear to enter that office one more time and in futility spend hours trying to get something done in an organization that was all politics. I had another career to pursue. I turned the car around and drove home. When I got home I phoned in my resignation.

"I quit my job," I said to the family at supper that night.

"You can't do that," Paul said. He was eleven now, and the effects of early rejection were beginning to show in him. I had tried often, with no success, to get his father to visit him. My hope was that being my own boss would give me the flexibility to spend more time with my sons.

"Yes, I can," I said. I glanced at Chip to see his reaction.

Chip just sliced away at the meat I had put on his plate. He didn't say anything, but I could see the annoyance on his face. "I just couldn't face that job one more day, so I came home. I called them later and told them I wouldn't be back. Somehow they weren't surprised."

"Somehow I'm not surprised, either," Chip said. Now he sent me one of those sour expressions I had grown to hate. "This is not exactly a news flash, your hating your job," he said. "I've seen this coming."

"And?"

"And you can't just quit a job," he said.

"Sure I can."

"It's irresponsible," he said. "We need the money. What makes you think it will be so easy to get another job?"

"I've already got one."

"Oh, you're not going to start again about raising kids being a job. I know it's work but it doesn't pay."

"It may be slow at first, but I'm going to open a practice as a private investigator."

"Oh, Jesus!"

"Oh, Jesus, yourself," I said. "I can do it. I'm going to specialize in finding missing people."

"Oh, great," Chip said. "I'm sure there's a big call for that."

"You'd be surprised at how many missing people there are," I said.

"Yes, I bet there's millions of missing people right here in Berne, huh? We probably even have a dozen or so down the cellar, right?"

"Not Berne. Albany," I said, glancing at Chip, reminding him of our conversation about my leaving.

"Marilyn, get realistic. How many cases do you think you can get out of Albany, Schenectady, and Troy? Or do you think millionaires are going to call you from Palm Springs and say 'Marilyn, I'm sending a satchel of cash over with a courier. I want you to fly down here right away and find my missing poodle'?"

Chip liked to laugh at his own jokes, and now he was more amused by himself than he was angry with me. Soon the kids started giggling, and even though I knew I was the butt of the joke, I smiled. It was nice to see everybody happy for a change.

A few weeks later I moved out. My departure was not quite the dramatic passage that it might seem. We talked about it. We agreed. My father was terminally ill and he needed me to take care of him. Paul and Joey and I moved into a small apartment in the same building with my father. At first, perhaps because we pretended it was not permanent, my leaving seemed to have no more emotional impact than the separation of roommates. Eventually, we got divorced.

In the early days of living without Chip I was stricken with a frightful loneliness. I must have missed him, but that wasn't all I was feeling. I deeply missed my mother, who now had been gone for more than six years. It seemed that my grief over her passing grew as time went on. Now, with my father suffering an incurable illness, I felt a persistent subtle uneasiness around me. When I would walk through the door of my apartment, I would feel as though someone were hiding there. I found myself looking under beds, opening closet doors, checking inside the shower each time, expecting to find an intruder. After several days of this I sat and thought, Marilyn, why are you doing this? You know there isn't anyone here. Just what is it that you are feeling? Thinking about it, I concluded, I'm feeling fear. I will be alone soon. My father fought his illness. He was determined that it wouldn't beat him, yet he wanted the suffering to end. I suffered with him. Then one day he gave up.

Chip had his own loneliness. After a few months he grew tired of living alone in the Berne house, so he moved to Albany, where he rented an apartment right across the street from us. Still, we saw little of him. Usually, if he came by, it was to talk to me or maybe spend some time with Joey. Chip had never been close to Paul. But Paul, the most sensitive member of the family, seemed to be the most wounded by Chip's absence.

One Saturday morning Chip came by to pick up some mail. Paul was outside playing ball. I went down to the street with Chip and watched him climb into his truck. Chip always kept the radio in the truck turned up so loud that he couldn't hear anything else. As he pulled away, Paul spotted him and went running after the truck. "Dad, Dad," he called. But Chip, with the radio turned up, couldn't hear Paul. As the truck disappeared around the corner, Paul just turned and looked at me sadly. "How come Dad never comes to see me?" he asked. "What did I do wrong?"

"Nothing, honey," I said, "you didn't do anything wrong." I held him in my arms, wiping the tears from his eyes and wondering which Dad he meant.

For my own loneliness there was only one antidote: work. For a while the office was quiet. I used those times to organize myself and make contacts in the investigation field. Then spare time became more and more rare as the phone began to ring a lot. But the calls weren't exactly what I had hoped for. Women called me and said things like, "My husband owes me seven thousand dollars in back alimony. If you can find him and get it out of him, I'll split it with you."

They called me to find their missing dog or cat. In fact, I got a lot of calls from people who told me they were certain their pet had been taken by a national dog-theft ring, which transported dogs coast-to-coast in vans.

Some calls were disturbing. One morning a man called up, mimicking an Indian accent.

"I want you to find my wife," he said. "She has run away with somebody."

After I wrote the details on the note pad I kept by the phone, the man said, "Where I come from we deal very sternly with this sort of thing. Would you deal sternly with her?"

"I'm not sure I understand," I said.

"I need to dispose of her," he said. "That is how we handle unfaithful wives where I am from."

"Well, that's not the way we do things in this country," I told him.

He hung up.

For a while I thought maybe I was being blessed with all these phone calls because I was female, so I called Scott Begun, another private detective, and asked him if his experience was similar.

"All of us get the crank calls," he said. "There's a lot of unstable people who take the TV image too seriously."

Scott told me he had taken his name off the lobby directory in his building because bizarre visitors constantly wandered into his office. They would sit and talk to him for a while, and then it would turn out there was a conspiracy to put them back in the hospital and they wanted him to crack the case just like Mike Hammer or Jim Rockford.

I learned quickly that this disturbing element was a part of the missing-person field. Sometimes husbands or wives leave because they find themselves trapped under the same roof with a crazy person. And sometimes people who are mentally troubled seek out the kind of notoriety that they think they can get from reporting a person missing.

In many cases the calls were legitimate, but I couldn't help. One man called me from Springfield, Massachusetts. After his divorce, his wife had gotten custody of one of their two daughters, and he had gotten the other. The wife had suggested that they each have a visitation day with both daughters. On her day she had taken the girls and fled.

As he told me the story I asked for the usual details—

wife's date of birth, motor-vehicle information, the children's last school, religion, all the things that would help me follow the paper trail.

After I had finished writing down this information, he said, "My wife's living in Puerto Rico now with her mother."

"You know where she is?" I asked with surprise.

"Oh, sure," he said. "I suspected she'd go there, so I called the house and my wife answered."

"Then she's not missing."

"Huh?"

"Your little girl, she's not missing," I said.

"Well, sure she is, she's in Puerto Rico," he said. "I need you to bring her back."

Many people just didn't understand that my job was to find missing people, not to bring people back. I soon realized that I would always hear from desperate people who hadn't made the distinction between a missing person and a person who was simply missing from their life.

When we first moved to Albany I lived very frugally. I spent time looking for discount coupons in the newspapers as well as planning meals around supermarket specials.

Although we had never had a lot of money, we had always been comfortable. Now their first bout with poverty was wearing on the children. One morning in the supermarket Paul kept picking up sweets, and I kept putting them down, saying, "No, honey, there's not enough money for extras." A moment would go by and Paul would disappear behind an aisle and come back with a box of cookies. Finally, I said, "Paul, will you listen to me. We cannot afford cookies. Not now."

"We could buy things when we lived with Daddy," Paul said in a child's way. The pouty look on his face conveyed the thought that he felt unloved. Children don't have the capacity to see things from an adult perspective. They don't worry about this month's rent; they only worry about cookies and to them that is very important.

I knew that my career had to take a turn for the better very soon. We had been living on supermarket specials far too long. When I got into the apartment the phone was ringing.

"Hello," a woman said. "Is this Marilyn Greene?"

"Yes."

"My name is Thelma Bartlett. I got your name from Scott Begun."

"How can I help you?" I asked.

"My husband is missing," she said.

The next day I drove up to Syracuse, New York, to see Thelma Bartlett. She was a middle-aged woman, tall and regal-looking. She had silvery hair with that blueish tint that had been popular years earlier. She reminded me of my third-grade teacher.

I sat at Thelma Bartlett's living-room table and she stood across from me with a basket of laundry in front of her. She folded laundry while we spoke, and every time she left the room to refill our coffee cups or answer the phone, I noticed that she did a chore along the way—brought a dirty dish back to the kitchen, straightened a book on the shelf, pressed a flower back into place in the vase that stood on the sideboard. "Never waste a step," she said proudly.

But clearly she was troubled by her husband's absence, and even while we talked the lines of worry seemed to deepen in her face.

"Ty just went to the convenience store to pick up some milk," she said. "He went for milk and bread and, you know, just a few things you need, and he never came back. The only odd thing about it, I mean at the time, was that he took the company car, which he normally only uses during the day at work. He didn't have to take it. The Pontiac is running fine."

"You called the police?"

"Yes. For a few days everybody was just baffled. There

was no sign of Ty, no sign of the car. Then the letters started coming."

She opened her pocketbook, which had been dangling from the arm of the chair where I sat, and she pulled out a packet of letters gathered together with a rubber band.

I read the letters while Mrs. Bartlett puttered around in the dining room. The first letter had been mailed from Binghamton, New York, which is near the Pennsylvania State line, about 75 miles south of Syracuse. "I can't come home," the letter said. "Something won't let me come back." The following day a letter had come from Watertown, New York, which is about 75 miles north of Syracuse. This one said, "I don't want to live." Then a letter came from Plattsburgh, up in the northeast corner of the state, 230 miles from Syracuse. The letter said, "I woke up this morning in Plattsburgh. I don't know how I got here." Then a letter came from Lake George, New York, then from Rochester, then Elmira. Then the letters stopped coming.

"Have you got a road atlas?" I asked Mrs. Bartlett.

"Why, yes, I suppose," she said. She headed for the bookcase in her living room, taking a pair of towels with her, which she folded along the way. She came back with the book of road maps.

"Ty was acting strangely for months before he left," she said. "I denied it at first, but I know it's true." While she told me about her husband, I put the letters in order and charted Mr. Bartlett's random route on the map. He had driven over a thousand miles, but he had never left the state.

Mrs. Bartlett told me that her husband was a fifty-year-old meeting planner for a large Syracuse corporation. He had been acting erratically for about a year but had somehow been able to manage his job. He had gone to a theater festival and walked onto the stage in the middle of a performance. He explained later that he had been daydreaming and had lost touch with where he was. Also, he had been getting up in the middle of the night and just sitting in the dark in the kitchen, and he had developed a number of neurotic habits, such as counting objects whenever he came into a room.

"And yet, he went to work every day," Mrs. Bartlett said. "He could function when he had to."

Mrs. Bartlett said her husband had always been subject to physical ailments due to mental stress. "Ty had colitis and an ulcer at age seven," she said. "His father is very wealthy; he owns a blacktop company and he never gave poor Ty any approval. Nothing Ty did was ever quite good enough."

"And what about now?" I asked. "Any special stress in the home?"

"Well," she said reluctantly, "our youngest son is having a minor problem with drugs." Quickly she added, "But our daughter Kate is going to college. She's doing fine."

When I was done with the interview I asked Mrs. Bartlett to give me the letters.

"Oh, I couldn't," she said. "Right now, they're all I have."

We drove to the post office, where I dropped coins into the photocopier while Mrs. Bartlett carefully placed each letter in the machine.

When I got home that night I read my copies of the letters more carefully. For the most part they rambled, and they were filled with frightening images and long delirious passages about unnamed anxieties. But in some there were spurts of lucidity, small paragraphs almost in another handwriting, about something as mundane as mowing the lawn. The letters seemed to have been written by two different people.

I took them to Dr. Alan Jacobs, an Albany psychiatrist whom I had met at Fran Poole's house. He shared my fascination with missing people and had offered to help if the occasion arose. Alan read the letters slowly in his office. Finally he looked up at me and said, "Marilyn, this is a very sick man."

"How sick?"

"It's very rare," he said, "but when you're dealing with a split personality you will have stories like these. This man is finding himself in situations and not knowing how he got there. One personality drove to Plattsburgh, another woke up there."

"Suicidal?" I asked.

"Quite possibly. Find him as soon as possible."

The police had not been searching for Bartlett because he had not been accused of any crime. The one hope I had of finding Mr. Bartlett quickly was to have police all over the state looking for him also. With Mrs. Bartlett's permission, I called Mr. Bartlett's employer and asked him to report the car as stolen.

Then I had Mrs. Bartlett call their bank and ask for their canceled checks and credit-card receipts. He had spent all the money in both accounts, but he was still writing checks and charging his motel rooms to his credit card. With the canceled checks and receipts I could chart his progress, though it could hardly be called *progress,* since he was zigzagging all over the state without any apparent pattern.

On a map at home I traced Mr. Bartlett's route back and forth across the state with a thick black marker. One night I taped the map to the wall of the living room—I had already begun to think of it as "my office"—then backed away from it and stared at it as if it would make more sense from across the room. On the tenth of the month Mr. Bartlett had been in Newburgh, New York. On the eleventh, Lake George again. On the twelfth he was in Ithaca. By the time the checks and receipts came in from these places, several days would have passed. Mr. Bartlett seemed to understand that he would be caught if he stayed in the same place for more than one night. And yet I was sure that he wanted desperately to be caught. He had stayed in the state of New York, as if afraid to go outside the familiar boundaries.

While I was studying the map, Paul and Joey came into the room. I knew they wanted me to play with them, and I knew I should, but I couldn't seem to take myself from the case.

"Mommy, what's that?" Joey asked.

"Oh, it's a kind of trail, honey, of a man I'm looking for."

Paul let out a big exaggerated groan.

"You're always working on something," he said.

His words were aimed right at my guilt. I knew I hadn't given the kids the extra attention they needed during this difficult time. The split from Chip, the illness of my father, and our lack of money were all piling on the stress. But this Bartlett case was an important assignment, and I wanted it to be a success.

"I'm sorry, boys," I said. "I tell you what, you want to help me with this case?" Although Paul had taken no interest in my work since the days when he had sat in trees waiting for Saki to find him, Joey, at seven, was already showing signs of being a future finder of missing people.

"So how come you can't find this guy?" Joey asked.

I smiled. "He's clever," I said. "He never stays in the same motel twice." We stood together staring at the map. "Except for Lake George," I said.

And then it struck me that there could be a pattern. I dashed back to the pile of receipts and checks I had left on the arm of the sofa. I pulled out the receipts from motels in Lake George. Mr. Bartlett had stayed in Lake George on the eleventh of the month and then again on the fifteenth, and again on the nineteenth and again on the twenty-third, three days ago.

"That's it," I said. My body felt charged with excitement. "He's not just staying at Lake George once in a while. He's staying there every fourth night."

"What does that mean?" Joey asked.

"It means there's a pattern to his movement," I said. Mr. Bartlett would be staying in Lake George that night. I was sure of it. I called the state police and told them of the case and my suspicion that Mr. Bartlett would be in a Lake George motel that night. I gave them a description and the plate number on the stolen car.

"Which Lake George motel?" the officer on the line asked.

"I don't know," I said. "He doesn't stay in the same motel twice."

"You don't know! Listen, lady," the officer said, "I'm not doing your investigation for you. You come up here and do it yourself." The conversation ended on that note.

In the years to come I would see this scene replayed many times over in different forms. Even though this man had been reported missing to the state police and was wanted for stealing a car, still it wasn't important enough for them to act on.

I then called the Lake George police and gave the same case background. I was pleased when they seemed interested in helping and agreed to look for the stolen vehicle.

There were twenty-five motels in Lake George at the time, and I had told the police they could skip the four Mr. Bartlett had already stayed in.

At two o'clock that morning the police pulled into the parking lot of the last motel on their list. To their surprise there was the stolen car. The police woke up the innkeeper, who opened the door with a key, and a groggy Mr. Bartlett gave himself up without incident.

Mr. Bartlett asked the police to take him to a hospital and said that he was happy the ordeal was over. He admitted to having sped through radar traps hoping to be stopped, and having gone through two police roadblocks thinking the police were looking for him, only to find that windshield registration stickers were being checked. After seeing the hospital psychiatrist, Mr. Bartlett agreed to a voluntary psychiatric admission.

When the police called me, I drove to Lake George to pick up Mr. Bartlett. He was pale and had a frightened look in his eyes. But, surprisingly, he was clean-shaven and had kept himself groomed and well dressed. He asked about his wife as we drove, but he spoke without passion, as though he were asking about somebody with whom he had gone to high school thirty years before. There was a hollow quality about the man, as though he had been tipped upside down and had all feelings shaken out of him. Most of the time he stared silently out the window of my car. I delivered him to a psychiatric clinic near his home.

That night I phoned Chip to tell him about the case and its outcome.

"You really found that guy?" Chip asked, sounding surprised.

"Yes."

"Gee," he said, "and you never even left your office."

That was the first I had realized that I hadn't left my office.

Late that night I thought of how the case really didn't have an ending. Mr. Bartlett was a troubled man and he had been located before doing any harm to himself. That in itself was a good ending. But what about his future? Would he recover from his illness and be a functional human being again? This question would never be answered for me. He had been located. My job was done.

9

Anne-Lee Scofield's daughter had been abducted by her ex-husband's parents. They had fought bitterly for custody in court, claiming Anne-Lee was not a fit mother.

"And they were right," Anne-Lee told me. She was a young woman, pretty, but she seemed to have done too much living too soon. "I can see that now. But that was five years ago. I've been working steadily for three years. I haven't had a drink. I want my baby back."

She pulled a manila envelope out of her pocketbook and dumped a sheaf of photocopy paper on my desk.

"They've been sending me copies of Beth's report cards, see, but the name of the school is torn off. Look at all those *A's*," she said, spreading the papers out in front of me. The report-card copies contained the girl's name, the subjects and grades, and a teacher's name. They had been mailed from Alabama, Mississippi, and Georgia, and I could tell from the subject list that Beth was in a public school. I looked at a map and saw that all the postmarks were from towns near the Tennessee State line. None had been mailed from Tennessee.

"Your daughter's in Tennessee," I said—and then, thinking I sounded a bit cocky, "I think."

I sent for a copy of the Tennessee school directory. When it came two weeks later I read through it page by page. I eventually came to the name of the teacher on the child's report card. By finding the school, I had found the child. It took one night. The girl had been missing for three years.

* * *

Ron Hite was a wealthy young man who pulled up in a Jaguar when we met to talk at a coffee shop in Albany. He bragged about earning two hundred thousand dollars a year in the wholesale lumber business, traveling to Canada and Oregon almost every week. Ron was immaculately dressed and groomed. Not a thread or a hair was out of place. Yet when he started to talk about his daughter, Lucille, his composure melted.

"I'm this big success," he said, "but I'd give it all up if I could have my daughter back. Her mother abducted her."

Ron and his wife had gone through what seemed to be a smooth divorce. They had been awarded joint custody of Lucille, who was eight at the time. But the mother had taken Lucille and moved away. Ron was able to send letters to his daughter through an aunt, who refused to reveal the location of the girl and her mother.

"When's your daughter's birthday?" I asked.

"November 12."

"Send her a postal money order for her birthday," I said. "Make it a big one so we can be sure it will be cashed. Two hundred dollars. Then we can trace it."

"We can?" He got excited. "Can we send it now?"

"It's risky," I said. "If it just comes out of the blue, your ex-wife might guess what you're up to, and she could drive several hundred miles to cash it. If it comes on the birthday, it will seem logical, and she'll cash it without suspicion."

Ron waited two months until the birthday, then he sent the money order. After enough time had passed for it to have been cashed, we went to the post office and filled out forms to have it traced; just as one would if it had been stolen. Within two weeks the tracer was complete and we knew that the money order had been cashed in Cranford, New Jersey. I checked the Cranford phone book and found the mother's name. Then I located the public school for her address and gave the information to

Ron Hite. Ron drove to Cranford and with police assistance took his daughter home with him.

Naomi Tieger had left her husband because she no longer wished to live within the constraints of an Orthodox Jewish home. She had gotten custody of their son, Samuel, even though her husband complained to the court that she would violate her agreement to bring up the boy in the Orthodox Jewish religion. The father, feeling strongly about his son's religious upbringing, had kidnapped the boy and taken him to Florida. Obviously, the father would enroll him in a Jewish school, so I told Naomi to send five dollars to the Florida Department of Education for a copy of their *Educational Directory for Nonpublic Schools*. "This directory lists every school by religious denomination," I explained.

After that, it was just a matter of calling the Jewish schools until she found the one Samuel was enrolled in.

Most of my early cases were parental abductions. Very few missing children are abducted by strangers. Most kids who are abducted are taken by a parent or another relative who was not given custody after a divorce, and my client was usually the parent who had legal custody. I found the children by following the paper trail that the abducting parent left behind. Virtually every resource I used—motor-vehicle records, school transcripts, postal forwards, trade certificates, employment reference letters, and so forth—were available to the searching parent as well as to me. But the parent didn't know what to look for or how to find it.

Often a parent came to me after his or her child had been missing two or three years, and often I would solve the case in a matter of days, using resources which had been readily available to the parent all the time.

With all my searches I kept careful records, and by the time I'd handled fifty cases, my apartment had all but disappeared under a blizzard of letters, file folders, reports, and hastily scribbled notes. For each client I typed a report on my old Royal portable. The report told the client where I had gone, who I saw, and what I learned. My copies went into loose-leaf notebooks, which I put on a shelf over my desk. Along with the final reports on cases I had solved, I had also accumulated a growing library of reports on unsolved cases, cases that in one way or another I would always be working on. Sometimes the reports were two pages, sometimes they were two hundred. I often fantasized about having a house of my own with an office that didn't have to double as a living room.

I found that, like search-and-rescue work, good private investigation required an open mind as well as a respect for probabilities. Each case was a lesson that could help me solve another case in the future. As my shelf began to bend under the weight of the reports, I saw that certain types of situations were more likely than others to cause a person to be missing.

In several cases, a person, usually a woman, had opted to leave a strict culture. Some of my clients were men who had brought their families to the United States from places in Asia or the Middle East, cultures where women are very oppressed. The stories were similar. The wives had gotten to America and, after observing our culture, said, "I don't have to live like a parcel of property any more if I don't want to." Some ran away. One heartbroken man from Pakistan looked me in the eye and sadly said, "I should never have let her go to college."

Love affairs, I found, were another frequent explanation for the sudden disappearance of an individual, usually married.

My first such case was the toughest. A man by the name of Paul Mahoney called and asked me if I could find his wife, Ellen. I drove to his apartment in Troy and spent two difficult hours in his living room. His lovely twelve-year-old daughter sat on the arm of the couch offering adult answers to my questions, while her grief-stricken father buried his face in his hands and wept.

Ellen had a job in the administrative office of a Troy hospital, the daughter told me. Lately she had been going to work earlier and coming home later.

"She was trying to earn more money because the bills have been piling up and Daddy's out of work," the girl explained. "Then, last Tuesday, she just never came home. She's been missing for five days."

"It isn't like Ellen to be even ten minutes late without phoning so that we won't worry," Mr. Mahoney said. It was unsaid, but I knew Mr. Mahoney was fearing the worst.

I went to the hospital to question some of Ellen's fellow workers.

"Look," her supervisor told me. He held up his thumb and index finger about a quarter of an inch apart: "Just between you and me, Ellen was that close to getting fired."

"Why?" I asked.

"She's been missing too many days. Leaving early. Coming in late. She's been warned several times."

Later, one of Ellen's co-workers took me aside and in conspiratorial tones informed me that Ellen had been having an affair with a hospital laundry worker named Cub. I went to the hospital laundry and found out that Cub had also stopped coming to work.

When I went to Cub's apartment, the landlady told me that he had moved out and that Cub's wife was home with their third baby.

As it turned out, Cub's wife knew about Ellen Mahoney.

"I'm looking for this woman," I said. I showed her Ellen's picture. "Have you seen her?"

"Is that the woman my Cub's been with?"

I didn't answer.

"She's not even very pretty."

"Do you know where they are?" I asked.

"Probably at his brother's house. He's gone there before with this woman."

She gave me the phone number, and when I called I spoke to Ellen Mahoney. She wasn't coming home, she said. She was happy, she said. Her husband and daughter could get along fine without her, she said.

When I told Paul Mahoney, he just said, "I understand." I think he knew deep down all along that he was living a lie, and now there was a decision he had to make.

Sometimes all I had to do was listen to a potential client and I would know immediately that a person had disappeared because he was living in a pressure cooker. There were many cases that I declined to handle because the would-be client was wild-eyed and frenzied. I shied away from other inquiring people without even seeing them when I sensed that the voice on the phone belonged to an angry or unstable person.

But there were times when I would not spot the instability right away. One well-groomed, soft-spoken woman came to me and asked me to find her two missing children. She seemed somewhat frantic as we talked, but that was understandable under the circumstances. Her husband had taken the children and abandoned her. It took me a month to find her children. When I telephoned the mother to tell her the good news, I was told that she had moved. It was hard to imagine a mother moving without giving her new address to the person who was searching for her children, but I began to search for her. Finding the mother turned out to be more difficult than finding the children. After two months, when I still hadn't located her, I got a letter from her saying that if I didn't find her children within thirty days she was going to have me killed. I thought, Well, Marilyn, this is an ideal mother; can't imagine why the husband fled.

As my confidence grew, I realized that I didn't have to be a wizard all the time. I made it a normal part of my practice, whenever possible, to teach clients how to find their own missing people. The mother of a missing child could often bring a lot more time, energy, and dedication to the search for her child than I could.

I would have been doing well economically if all these people were paying clients. But they weren't. Much of my time was taken up with pro bono cases. I learned quickly that families with missing members are, to a large extent, those with broken homes, the poor, the mentally ill; families that are disfunctioning from drug abuse, alcoholism, or incest. I never rejected or resented searching parents who happened to be poor. They still needed the help, and I could hear them crying deep inside. What amazed and intrigued me were the economically well-off families who would balk at even very modest fees.

In one instance I accepted for a fee of five hundred dollars the case of a fifteen-year-old girl who had been missing over a year. After two months of part-time work on the case, I arranged to have the girl's picture printed in a national magazine. There had been no publicity about her disappearance, and I felt that the exposure could be what the case needed. As it turned out, the girl was living in Nebraska with her boyfriend. The boyfriend's mother saw the magazine and insisted that the girl call home. The girl's parents called me and asked for their five hundred dollars back. When I asked why, they said, "Well, Mrs. Greene, you didn't find her. She was found because of the magazine."

On another case, an older couple hired me to find their twenty-seven-year-old son, a mental-hospital outpatient who had walked out of a party and hitchhiked out of state. After listening to the particulars of the case, I suggested an initial retainer of fifteen hundred dollars.

"Well, isn't that quite a lot of money for this sort of thing?" the father asked.

"No," I said. "Some investigators would ask you for twenty-five thousand."

"What are you going to spend it on?"

"On finding your son," I said.

He stared at me and waved a hand in the air, inviting me to explain further.

"Telephone calls," I said, "postage, stationery, registry of motor-vehicle fees, gasoline, typewriter ribbons, medical school."

"Medical school?" he asked. I had caught him by surprise.

"That's one of the things you're paying for when you pay your doctor's bill," I said, "the years he spent learning how to treat your ulcer. I've spent years learning my profession, too."

After I had spent a month on the case and paid my own expenses, I located their son in a Baptist mission in New Orleans. Because he was terrified of flying, I arranged for him to be put on a bus with an escort and returned to New York. A week later, I got a formal letter from the father requesting a portion of the money back. He wrote: "Since you couldn't possibly have used up the entire fifteen-hundred-dollar retainer, please return to me the unused portion."

In my accounting to him I had listed several long-distance phone calls. He referred to four of them, which he said I had never made. He must have had a friend with the phone company, who reviewed my phone bill. Apparently, it hadn't occurred to him that I might have made those calls from other phones. I didn't want an unhappy client, so I sent him a check.

I was continually amazed and frustrated by the number of people who seemed to think a private investigator should work for free. One morning after I spent hours bent over my checkbook, trying to shorten the pile of unpaid bills, I called Scott Begun. He had been my professional ally, always there with a tip or a few words of support.

"Scott, how do you make a living at this?"

"Insurance companies," he said. "Worker's-compensation

cases. That's how I make most of my income, proving that some people who put in disability claims are fakers. When I catch someone, it saves the insurance company a fortune in benefit payments. They routinely have outside private investigators handle their cases, but you have to be good."

Scott had plenty of business, and he offered to farm some of it out to me. I thanked him but told him I didn't think I'd be good at that sort of thing. The truth was I had never wanted to be a general private investigator. I just wanted to find missing people. The problem was that it wasn't paying enough, and I was behind in my bills.

A few weeks later, however, when I was going to Texas to visit my brother, I called Scott. I thought if there were some work down there for me, it might at least help pay for the trip.

"Got anything in Dallas?" I asked.

As it happened, he did. A construction worker from Albany had tumbled off a ladder and had gone on worker's compensation, claiming that his spine had been seriously injured and he could no longer do heavy labor. The insurance company had received a tip that the man was installing fences for a small company in the Dallas area. They needed proof.

During the first evening at my brother's house we were eating dinner, when I was suddenly surprised by my brother's voice. "Marilyn, what case are you working on now?" he asked. He had caught me daydreaming when he was speaking to me.

"Oh, sorry," I said. What surprised me was the realization that I had been thinking about the worker's-compensation case. Would I catch this guy working? How would I keep him from seeing me? How much proof would I need? What would be my cover story if he caught me? I told my brother about the case and he smiled and asked, "How can I help?"

"Tell me how to get to Irving," I said. "The Plymouth Park Shopping Center."

Early the next morning I drove to the Every Kind Fence Company, which was near the shopping center. That's where the insurance claimant, Hower Lister, was allegedly working. I parked across the street from the back of the building where the trucks were kept. It was still early and the company had not yet opened. I studied my description of Lister. Six-foot even. A hundred and seventy-five pounds. Shaggy blond-brown hair. Blue eyes. A mustache.

By 8:00 A.M. the sounds of men at work began to echo inside the tin-roofed building. At a few minutes before nine two men came out and climbed into a truck that had apparently already been loaded for them. One of the men was about six feet tall, with shaggy blond hair and blue eyes. It's got to be Lister, I thought. When the truck pulled out, I followed.

The truck led me to a peaceful suburban neighborhood where all the houses looked alike and station wagons were parked in most of the driveways. As the streets grew more and more residential I began to get edgy. Two more turns, I thought, and it will be obvious that I'm following them. Just when I was ready to turn a different way to avoid being detected, the fence company's truck pulled up in front of a house that looked like the others, except that a huge fallen tree was sprawled across the front lawn. The tree had crashed through a fence and sheared a metal basketball post nearly in half. The heavy metal backboard and the top half of the post dangled almost to the ground.

I parked my car half a block behind them, on the other side of the street, hoping that no neighbors would notice me. I pulled a road map out of the glove compartment and spread it in front of me so that I would appear to be lost, if someone did take an interest in me. I was armed with a 35-millimeter camera and a telephoto lens. The two men from the fence company hadn't even noticed me.

For two hours they worked on clearing the tree out of the way. Using chain saws, they sliced the trunk into ten or twelve huge logs. I took pictures. My man looked as healthy as a horse to me, but I didn't think cutting a tree with a chain saw proved he was strong enough for heavy labor.

When they were done cutting, the men rolled away the logs, which must have weighed a hundred pounds each. I took more pictures, but they still wouldn't prove anything. Both men rolled each log, so it was impossible to determine who was doing the work. From time to time it occurred to me that I could be wasting my time. My man might not do anything to prove he was fit for hard labor, and even if he did, I didn't know for sure that he was Hower Lister.

When the logs were gone, the men began pulling out the old fence and tossing the rotted pickets aside. How strenuous would replacing the fence be, I wondered. Would it be arduous enough to prove this man was a fraud? I doubted it.

While they were working, a woman came out of the house, carrying two glasses of lemonade. She gave each man a glass. Fortunately, she was young and attractive, because as soon as she started frowning and gesturing toward the broken basketball post, my subject walked over to it.

He stared at it for a few minutes and poked it with his hand, perhaps wondering how he could cut through the inch or so of jagged, unsheared metal that kept the top half of the post and backboard from falling off. Then suddenly he grabbed the backboard with both hands and reared back and began twisting it back and forth as though he were steering a huge truck around sharp curves. Finally, after he had worked himself into a sweat, the pole snapped off with a cracking sound that I could hear half a block away, and he triumphantly tossed the whole broken contraption into the back of his truck as though it were no heavier than a toolbox. I got pictures of everything.

Two weeks later I was at home when Scott Begun called.

"Marilyn, great pictures," he said.

"Thanks," I said. "But were they of the right person?" I held my breath.

"They were Lister, all right. Your check is on the way. The company is very happy with your work. I gave them your phone number. I think they'll send some business your way."

I was smiling when I hung up the phone. I knew that finding missing people would always be my first love, but it was nice to know I had found something that would pay the rent.

10

"I don't get it," Frances Eldman said. "I just don't get it."

She was about sixty years old, with big, sad eyes.

Frances lived on a tree-lined street outside of Baltimore, in a three-story apartment building that was owned by her thirty-year-old son, Mark Eldman, who had disappeared a week ago. When Frances had seen my picture in the paper, she called, and I drove down to see her.

"It just doesn't make any sense," Frances Eldman said again, shaking her head. We were in Mark's apartment on the third floor, five gorgeously decorated rooms drenched in sunshine on this lovely Saturday morning. Mark's Porsche was still in the driveway below. Frances led me through the apartment while we talked.

I could see that the young man had been fastidious. Nothing was out of place, nothing seemed to be missing. I pulled his bank passbook out of a dresser drawer and glanced at it. He had saved several thousand dollars.

"Look," Frances said, taking a neatly folded hundred-dollar bill from a small ceramic bowl on the dresser. "He didn't even take his emergency hundred."

"Has he been depressed lately?" I asked.

"No," she said. "His job is going well. He was even getting ready to buy another building. I asked Danny if he knew of anything that might be troubling Mark, anything that would make him want to get away, but there was nothing."

"Who's Danny?"

"Danny Bellino," she said. "Mark's best friend. He lives across the street. Nice boy. They had a terrible fight a few nights before Mark disappeared, and I thought that might have had something to do with it. But Danny says no."

"What did they fight about?"

"Who knows?" she said. "They fight a lot. Mark spends a lot of time at Danny's apartment, but lately Danny's got a new girlfriend and he doesn't have much time for Mark."

"I see," I said.

We went back up to Frances Eldman's apartment, where I had set my portable typewriter on her kitchen table. I asked her to tell me as much as she could about Mark, and while she talked I typed notes and asked occasional questions.

When I finished my interview, I walked across the street to Danny Bellino's apartment and introduced myself to him. He was a slim, brown-haired, soft-spoken young man. I told him who I was and that I was looking for his friend. Wearing a T-shirt and blue jeans, Danny stood barefoot in the doorway to his apartment, politely answering my questions but not inviting me to enter. When my questions continued long enough for our hallway conversation to feel uncomfortable, he suggested that I give him five minutes and meet him in the yard behind the house.

"It's nice out," he said, "we can talk there."

While I stood out in the backyard waiting for Danny, I analyzed my assumptions about thirty-year-old men who still live at home, who are fastidious, who have fights with close male friends. Being a woman in a man's field, I don't care much for stereotypes, but there wasn't much point in lying to myself. Right or wrong, I suspected that Mark and Danny were lovers.

By the time Danny met me in the yard he had shaved

and combed his hair. He came down the back stairs from his apartment wearing a fresh shirt, a blue blazer, dress pants, and well-shined loafers.

"Sorry if I was rude," he said. "My girlfriend was there. It would have been awkward."

For several minutes he talked about his girlfriend, Jeannie, and how great it felt to be in love.

When I asked about Mark, Danny turned his face from me.

"I heard you guys had a fight," I said.

"Oh, sure. But we got it straightened out," Danny said. "Right here." He turned and pointed to a spot in the grass. "We sat in the yard and talked, and then we walked for a while. That was the last time I saw him."

"Where did you walk?"

"Oh, you know, just around the yard here."

Danny and I started walking. The yard was several times as wide as the building that stood on it, and the grass was overgrown. There was no fence, but at the end of the yard there was a densely wooded area that quickly grew dark where the tangled layers of leafy branches held back the sunlight. It was an intriguing spot, the kind of place where children dream away the hours playing enchanted forest. We moved slowly toward it.

"Mark is my friend," Danny said, "but sometimes he is not very nice."

"What do you mean?"

"Well, sometimes he can be, I don't know... arrogant. Even cruel."

"Give me an example," I said.

"I mean, like he owns those apartments and he's thrown people out on the street because they got fired and couldn't pay their rent on time. Nice people, too. Not deadbeats. I could never do that."

"Are you saying that somebody could have hurt Mark to get even for something?" I asked.

"Could be," Danny said. Then: "Oh, I don't know. With

Mark you never know. He probably just went off someplace to have a good time and didn't tell anybody."

We reached the woods at the end of the yard. I kept moving forward, stepping onto a path of beaten-down grass that worked its way between the trees. Danny turned left abruptly before we could enter the woods. I felt his hand tugging urgently at my elbow.

"We went this way," he said.

At that moment I knew I was walking with a murderer.

I could feel it. This had been the last walk Mark Eldman had ever taken. I knew that something terrible had happened in those woods. I knew that Danny didn't want to take me to the place where he had murdered his best friend.

I moved slowly along beside Danny, not frightened but cautious. I didn't want to push the button that could make Danny feel threatened. I let him talk.

"Mark had a lot of good qualities," he said. "I'm not saying he didn't. But he could be domineering and really selfish. I guess what I'm trying to say is that, sure, it would be awful if anything happened to Mark, but it's not like he was this wonderful person or anything."

For a long time Danny talked about Mark, always in the past tense. His mood seemed to shift from light to dark to light again, and by the time we said goodbye he seemed remarkably cheerful.

I stayed at a motel that night, reading over my typewritten notes. Mark and Danny, I suspected, were lovers at one time. But now Danny had a girlfriend and that made for a volatile situation. Danny had murdered Mark, I was sure of it. And yet I was equally sure that Danny was a gentle person, not a hardened criminal. Danny, I felt, was someone who would not be capable of murder unless he were pushed very hard.

Early the next morning I parked at the end of Danny's street and worked my way through the woods that ran along the length of the block. When I got to the area behind Danny's house, I searched. It felt odd to be in there searching without a dog. But I wasn't looking for a body.

Danny Bellino had not impressed me as the sort of young man who could plan a murder, purchase a gun, carefully choose his time and place, and then coldly cover up the evidence. I was sure that whatever had happened in those woods had happened suddenly and passionately.

After five minutes I found what I was looking for. Small specks of dried blood were splattered against the base of a birch tree. There had been a lot more blood, I was sure, but it had been absorbed by the soil.

It was time to call the police.

I spoke to a Detective Sorensen, and he asked me to step away from the case.

"We need a body," he said, "or there will never be a conviction."

Danny Bellino was put under surveillance, and I drove home, not yet able to tell Frances Eldman that her son, almost surely, had been murdered by his best friend.

I might have stayed in Baltimore a few days longer, but I had a Monday-night appointment to keep on another case.

A woman by the name of Shirley Tarle had come to me because her sixteen-year-old daughter, Cheryl, and another girl had run away from a center for wayward girls. Cheryl had been a problem for two years, so Mrs. Tarle had gotten a PINS ("person in need of supervision") petition from the court to put Cheryl in the center. It wasn't until after Cheryl ran away that the mother realized what she had signed.

"They won't look for Cheryl," she had told me on the phone. "They won't let me look at my own daughter's file; they won't even tell me the name of the girl she ran away with. It's like Cheryl's not even my daughter, anymore. She's theirs."

So on Monday night after I returned from Baltimore I

left my boys with a sitter and I went with Mrs. Tarle to the center to see the director. The director was a small woman who wore a gray business suit and sensible shoes. Her office was so neat it looked as if she had never used it. Marilyn, I told myself, this is a woman who probably has never done anything in her life that wasn't by the book.

"I think I can find Cheryl if you give me the name of the girl she ran away with," I told her.

"That information is confidential," she said. "I have already explained that to Mrs. Tarle." She pressed her lips together. "Several times," she added.

"Well, I'm sure that if you put us in touch with the parents of the other girl, they would be happy to permit you to give us the information we need."

"Mrs. Greene," she said, "if I were to put you in touch with the parents of the other girl, then I would be identifying her and violating that confidentiality, now wouldn't I?"

Mrs. Tarle, sitting next to me, was red-faced and ready to scream. "Please," I said to the director, "I'm sure the parents of the other girl are as desperate for information as Mrs. Tarle is."

She smiled insincerely. "If I broke the rules every time a girl ran away, there wouldn't be any point to the rules, now would there?"

"Could we try this," I said, "could you call the parents of the other girl and tell them the mother of the girl their daughter ran away with wants to speak to them? Ask them if they will give you permission to tell us who they are."

"That," she said, "would not be proper procedure in a situation like this."

"Well, what is proper procedure?" I asked.

"I don't know."

"Well, it's your job to know," I said somewhat impatiently.

The director pursed her lips, looked at Mrs. Tarle, then back at me.

"Possibly I could make an inquiry such as the one you suggest," she said. "However, it will take time."

"Time?" I asked. "What time? You pick up the phone and dial the number."

"That won't do," she said. "I am required to get their permission in writing."

"Oh, god!" I said, in disbelief.

It took three days for the director to get signed permission from the other girl's parents. Three days, during which anything could have happened to Cheryl.

I called the girl's parents and they told me their daughter was living with her boyfriend. I called the daughter and asked her if she knew where Cheryl was.

"Cheryl? Sure, she's hooking at the Rose Lounge," the girl said, as if being a prostitute were as routine as waiting on tables.

The Rose Lounge was in a town less than fifty miles away. I called the police there and told them that a minor girl was engaged in prostitution at the Rose Lounge, and that she was a runaway. Could she be picked up and held until her mother could get there? They told me in so many words that they couldn't do that and, besides, they had never heard of the Rose Lounge.

When I found Cheryl she was perched on a stool at the Rose Lounge, looking not a day over sixteen and hustling drinks. She was proud to tell me how it worked.

"See, I just sit with a guy," she said, "and he buys drinks for both of us. Drinks cost three bucks each. Except mine is really just ginger ale, and Larry, he's the bartender, he gives me a ticket for every drink I hustle, and at the end of the night I turn in my tickets for fifty cents each."

Cheryl wasn't as quick to brag about the prostitution. She was relieved that I had come to take her home. When we got to her house, Cheryl and her mother hugged and talked for a long time. By the time I left them, things looked hopeful, and I drove home thinking this is what I dreamed about when I was in search-and-rescue.

The Rose Lounge, incidentally, was next door to the police station.

The day after I brought Cheryl home I got a call from Detective Sorensen in Baltimore. I was surprised to hear his voice. Unlike the police on television, real-life police don't make it their practice to inform private investigators of the progress of a case. But Sorensen was different.

"The state police pulled Mark Eldman's body out of Chesapeake Bay," he said.

"Today?"

"Would you believe six days ago?" he said. "It seems that nobody got around to reading the Teletypes until today."

"Did he die of knife wounds?"

"Yes. Danny Bellino's being charged with murder. You'll probably have to testify."

I spent the next couple of days feeling somewhat depressed over the probable fate of Danny Bellino. I knew that going to the police was the right thing to do, but it occurred to me that Danny's punishment would result from a choice I had made, and I felt the weight of that choice.

I was learning that there were a lot of tough choices to be made in this field. The private-investigation profession is not known for its high ethical standards, and I had to establish my own rules as I went along. In some cases, I didn't even know what the rule was until I was confronted with the need to make a decision.

One such case involved a man by the name of Harvey MacKay who came to my house one night on a motorcycle. MacKay was overweight, silver-haired, and at age fifty-five he was dressed like a twenty-year-old kid.

"It's my daughter I want to find," he said. "Karen. About two years ago she just broke off all communication with me. But I'd still like to see her."

MacKay was a machinist, a partner in a small company that made molds for tools manufactured by big companies. He popped antacids into his mouth one after the other, as if they were candy.

"Reflux," he explained. "It's a stomach thing, caused by stress. I never had stress when I was just a machinist. It ain't the work that causes it; it's owning the company. Knowing you got to meet a payroll and pay the bills, that's what causes stress."

I nodded. I could certainly relate to that even though finances had gotten much better since I'd started getting cases from insurance companies and I was saving money for a down payment on a house for the boys and me.

MacKay spent a lot of time talking about things that didn't seem to have anything to do with his missing daughter. He joked about everything in his life and laughed nervously.

"See, the wife and I got divorced a couple years back," he finally said. "I'm remarried now. And I want to have some contact with my daughter, Karen. That's all, I just want to see her once in a while."

"Where do you think she is?"

"Oh, she's somewhere in the tri-city area," he said. "Somebody seen her shopping one time in Albany."

"Why do you suppose she's rejected you?" I asked.

"I don't know. It must have been something her mother told her."

He seemed surprisingly incurious about what that might be.

The next day I made a pretext phone call to Karen's mother. I told her I was Jennifer Cavilleri, an old school chum of Karen's, and I needed Karen's current address for a reunion. It was a dumb name to use. Jennifer Cavilleri is the character in the book *Love Story,* and there was a chance that Karen's mother was one of the millions who had read it.

The mother didn't seem to recognize the name, but she

did say, "Gee, Jennifer, I don't recall Karen ever mentioning your name." It was obvious that she suspected something.

I knew she would visit her daughter sooner or later, so I decided to watch her house.

One day Joey went with me. We spent hours parked down the street from Mrs. MacKay's split-level ranch house. Joey and I played the same card games I had played with Paul when he was smaller. Joey thought the funniest thing in the world was to switch the cards around whenever I looked up to make sure Mrs. MacKay's car was still parked in her driveway.

"Now, did you cheat while I wasn't looking?" I would ask.

"Oh, no, Ma. I would never do that," Joey would say, and the edges of his lips would rise in just the slightest smile that he would be trying to hold back.

"Are you sure?"

"Pretty sure," he would say, and the smile would spread across his face.

"Absotively?"

"Absotively," he would say. And when he couldn't hold back anymore, his entire body would convulse and he would be transformed into a quivering blob of giggly little boy.

Joey and I followed Mrs. MacKay to the grocery store and the dry cleaners and the Salvation Army thrift shop, and every place else she went for two nights.

On the third night I left Joey with a sitter. At eight o'clock that night, Mrs. MacKay pulled out of her driveway and headed toward Albany. She led me downtown to a brick apartment building. I pulled into a parking lot across the street and watched her go in. Let it be Karen's, I thought. I didn't want to spend another week sitting in the car every night.

An hour later Mrs. MacKay came out of the building. After she drove off I crossed the street and checked the mailboxes in the hallway. There was the name K. MacKay.

I took the elevator up. A slim young woman with reddish hair and freckles answered my knock.

"Karen MacKay?" I asked.

"Yes."

"My name is Marilyn Greene," I said slowly, while maintaining eye contact. "I'm a private investigator."

"My father sent you?" she asked.

"Yes."

"Come in."

It was a small apartment, three rooms, not luxurious but cozy. As I glanced around I felt a strong sense of Karen's independence.

We sat in Karen's kitchen, which was cluttered with open textbooks.

"I take some courses," Karen explained, pushing the books aside and making space for a pair of coffee mugs.

I have noticed over the years that while men can take forever to say something personal, women often go directly to matters of the heart. Before Karen had even poured my coffee, she was telling me about her childhood. It was what I had suspected.

"My father was molesting me for as far back as I can remember," she said. "He never beat me. He wasn't violent. Just intimidating. Whenever my mother was out he would invite me to join him upstairs...at a 'party,' he called it."

"Your mother never suspected?" I asked.

"I don't know," Karen said. "Sometimes I think she must have known but just didn't want to face it. I mean, normally, we never locked our front door. But my father always locked the door when the two of us were alone upstairs. It seems impossible that my mother never noticed that the only time she ever came home to a locked house was when my father and I were home alone. Anyhow, the parties always became sexual. I never felt as if I had any choice."

"When did it end?"

"When I was sixteen. I still couldn't confront him directly. Even now, I haven't. But I left him a note that said, 'I don't want to go to any more parties.' He never bothered me again. But he never acknowledged all those years of abuse either, and I can't forgive him for that."

Karen told me that by the time she was eighteen years old she couldn't bear to be in the same room with her father.

"So I left," she said. "Went to California for a while. Came back. Now I've got a job." She smiled. "A boyfriend." She smiled again. "And a therapist!"

"What will you do if your father finds you?" I asked.

"I'll have to move again."

As I got ready to leave, she asked the question that had hung in the air since I'd arrived. "Are you going to tell him where I am?"

"No," I said. I didn't give it a lot of thought. It just came out, and in that moment I had established one of the rules for my own professional life. When I find an adult who doesn't want to be found, I don't tell the client where he is. I take a photograph and I ask for a handwritten note so that I can show the client the missing person is alive and well. But that's all. It seems to me that a sane, law-abiding adult has the right to remain lost.

As it happened, my scruples were to be tested more severely a dozen or so cases later.

The client was an Iranian man named Adel. Adel was a surgeon, and I was referred to him by Dr. James Bartlett, the brother of the man who had zigzagged all over New York State. Adel called to tell me his fifteen-year-old daughter had disappeared, and we made arrangements for me to interview him.

He had taken his family and fled Iran when the Ayatollah took over. Apparently he had quite a bit of wealth, because his mansion overlooking Long Island Sound would have done nicely as a palace.

When I arrived I pulled up in the gravel driveway, walked past the heated swimming pool and through the French doors where Adel met me in a marble entrance hall that was furnished with silk-covered chairs, a crystal chandelier, and pots of flowers. The hall was bigger than my apartment.

Adel was a stunning, middle-aged man with a small black beard and intelligent, seductive brown eyes. His shoes clicked musically on the white marble floor as he led me into the living room, where another chandelier reflected light in a mirror over the marble fireplace. I sat in a large, regal-looking chair. He sat on a couch and he looked me over.

"You are a woman," he said, as if he were just discovering it, even though he had called me.

"Yes," I said.

"Tell me," he said, "your husband allows you to do this?"

I didn't answer. There didn't seem to be any point in getting into my personal life or discussing the implications of the word "allow."

Adel shook his head. "You'll excuse me."

"If you are uncomfortable with a female investigator, I will understand," I said.

He smiled. "Dr. Bartlett says you are the best. I always get the best."

Adel's wife entered the room quietly and sat beside her husband on the couch. Together they told me about their daughter Roya.

Roya had been acting strangely for a few days before she disappeared. She had not been eating, and she seemed to be constantly distracted. She was enrolled at a private school in West Islip, and when the family chauffeur drove to pick her up after school on the previous Tuesday, she had not been there to meet him.

In some ways, conducting the interview was like having

a conversation in Grand Central Station. Grandmothers, sisters, brothers, uncles, cousins, and god knows who else crossed the wide tiled floor of the living room while we spoke. This was an extended family, and every new refugee from the Ayatollah's Iran had been made welcome. I didn't know if I was getting to see so many family members because this room was a passage to every other room in the house or because they were all trying to get a look at the lady detective.

I spent much of the afternoon with Roya's parents. I wanted to know her background. Who were her friends? What were her hobbies? How were her marks in school? Roya, it seemed, led a life that placed her in constant conflict between the normal activities of a teenaged American girl and the demands of her Islamic upbringing. When I asked which boys she'd had dates with, the parents stared at me as if I had recently arrived from another planet.

"Dates?"

"Yes," I said, "with boys."

Adel let out a hearty laugh. "You excuse me, Mrs. Greene, but we are still Iranians. Some day we will go back to our country and Roya will be married. There will be no . . ." He paused and smiled again as if he were about to reveal the punch line to a very clever joke: "dates," he said, and he could barely keep himself from laughing.

While we sat in the living room the phone next to the couch rang twice. Both times Adel's wife picked it up, spoke briefly in Persian, and then made a face. Apparently somebody was hanging up.

Later Adel, his wife, and I walked into the kitchen and sat at a long table where Roya's older sister served us tea. Afterwards, Adel excused himself to go upstairs for photos of Roya to give me. While he was gone, the phone rang again. The sister answered. She spoke Persian and edged her way into a pantry, closing the door behind her. Since she was speaking a language that I didn't understand, I was sure she wasn't trying to keep the conversation private from me. If she didn't want her parents to hear, it must be a boy, I thought. Or Roya.

She hung up the phone and came out of the pantry before her father returned. A few minutes later, while Adel was dropping dozens of photos of Roya on the table, the older sister appeared in the kitchen. She was carrying a gym bag. She spoke to Adel in Persian, then left.

I got up from my chair. "Is she going out?" I asked Adel.

"Yes," he said, placing an arm around his wife. "Mrs. Greene, we don't keep our daughters in prison."

"I must go," I said. I scooped the photographs from the table and shoved them into my pocketbook.

"Now?" he asked.

"Yes, I'll call you later," I said.

By the time I got to my Volkswagen, the older sister was turning left out of the long driveway in her Mercedes.

I followed her for about two miles, and she pulled into the horseshoe-shaped driveway of another house, not as palatial as her own but still luxurious.

I drove slowly past the house, stopped just beyond the other end of the horseshoe, and watched her through the rearview mirror.

She didn't go into the house. She went around it, clutching the gym bag and glancing around as if she were about to commit a crime.

I got out of my car and walked across the lawn. I had no idea how I would explain my trespassing if anybody asked, but I was ninety-percent certain that I was about to find Roya, and that was worth the ten-percent chance of looking like an idiot. The back lawn stretched to the edge of an inland waterway. Docked to a pair of wide wooden posts was a fifty-foot yacht.

I walked to the end of the yard. The yacht hugged a wall that rose about ten feet above the water. From where

I stood I could hear two female voices and a male talking in the lower-deck cabin.

"Permission to come aboard," I shouted. I had no idea what I was dealing with. Scared people sometimes do crazy things when you come barging in on them. One thing was certain, however; no one was getting off that boat unnoticed.

Silence.

I waited. Finally, the older sister appeared at the door to the cabin. Looking stunned but with no other alternative, she motioned for me to come aboard.

I climbed on deck, and without speaking she led me down into the cabin. The cabin, with plush white carpeting and highly polished wood everywhere, was as luxurious as Adel's house had been. Roya sat on a small, leather-covered couch. The young man with her was American, probably not much older than Roya. They held hands and stared at me meekly, as if they were about to be arrested.

The two women spoke to each other in Persian and then the sister turned to me.

"She wants to know if you are going to tell our father where she is."

"I'm afraid I have to," I said. "She's still a minor."

"But you don't understand," the sister said. She spoke again in Persian. Roya nodded.

"She is pregnant," the sister said.

"I know it will be difficult," I said, "but running away won't solve the problem of a pregnancy. Can this be worked out with your parents?"

"No," the older sister said. "Iranians don't work things like this out. In our culture Roya can never be married. She is not a virgin."

I glanced at the young man. He said nothing.

"Roya is only fifteen," she said. "Besides, Sean is an American."

"Look," I said, speaking directly to Roya, "I can't make you come with me. But you're a minor and your parents are very worried. They have trusted me to try to find you. I have to tell them where you are."

Roya looked at me. She had her father's eyes. Again her sister spoke for her.

"You will tell them she is pregnant, that she is in love?"

"No," I said. "They hired me to find Roya and that's what I've done."

The four of us sat in that cabin for hours discussing Roya's fears and the many approaches that she could take with her family. Roya wanted the understanding and support of her mother, but she feared disappointing her family and being shunned. At the end of the day, Roya had made some difficult but mature decisions with which she was comfortable. Then she agreed to let me take her home.

After driving back to Adel's house with Roya, I headed for home. The next night Adel called me. For several minutes he made awkward small talk, asked about my kids, talked about the weather. Finally, after a pause, he asked me if I had ever delivered ransom to recover a kidnap victim.

"No," I said. "It's never come up."

"Is it the sort of thing you would do?"

"I suppose it is," I said. I couldn't see what he was getting at.

"Mrs. Greene," he said, and he seemed to be choosing his words one at a time, "I would like you to deliver ransom money for my daughter Roya. You will come here and pick up five thousand dollars."

"But Roya hasn't been kidnapped," I said.

"Yes, I know," he said. "She is back on that yacht where you found her. But, Mrs. Greene, you must understand our culture. What Roya has done is a shameful matter to us. We have decided to send her to school in France, at least until the child is born. But an explanation is needed for our friends and family."

"You want to tell them she was kidnapped?"

"Yes," he said. "That would not be a shameful matter."

"Then why not just tell them she was kidnapped?" I asked.

Adel chuckled. "Iranians are suspicious people," he said. "But if our community were to see you leave the house with the money, and see Roya come home, they would not be so suspicious and there would not be gossip."

"I don't think I can help you," I said.

"Mrs. Greene, I hope that I am making myself clear. Once you have left my home with the five thousand dollars, you do not have to come back."

"I see," I said.

It was tempting. I had vivid images of what I could buy with the money. Certainly it would help with the down payment on a house. But equally vivid were my images of men from the New York State Attorney General's office or the FBI pounding on my door. This was the kind of thing that could cost a private investigator her license.

"I cannot help you," I said, knowing that with five thousand dollars to spend, Adel would have no trouble finding another private investigator to run his errand.

It was a cold day in Baltimore when I testified at the murder trial of Danny Bellino.

It was a sad day in many ways. Even though Mark Eldman was dead, nobody stood up to say that he was a fine young man or that his death was a terrible loss. It seemed that everybody, except his mother who sat in the back of the courtroom weeping into a handkerchief, thought Mark Eldman was a first-class bastard.

In soft, somber tones Danny told the court that he had been having an affair with Mark. He had tried to get out of it several times, he said, but Mark would not let him. Mark bullied him and threatened to expose that Danny was gay to Danny's parents and boss. And each time that Mark threatened, Danny gave in to the emotional blackmail.

And then Danny met Jeannie. When he fell in love with her, he wanted to put his past behind him. He began to question whether he had ever really been gay at all. He told Mark he had to end their relationship.

"I pleaded with him that morning," Danny said. "I told him we could still be friends. But he refused. He taunted me. He said he was going to tell Jeannie that I was his lover. He didn't really even feel bad about it. He liked the idea of exposing me and he kept saying over and over that he was going to tell Jeannie and everybody that I was gay; and I kept telling him I wasn't really gay, and he kept saying I was, and finally I just . . . couldn't take it anymore. So I punched him to the ground in the woods and then I jumped on him. He picked up a rock and started hitting me with it. I was so angry that I just . . . started stabbing him with the pocket knife I always carry."

I walked away from the courthouse that day thinking about how many lives are crushed by a tragedy. Frances Eldman had lost a son. Jeannie had lost a love. Mark Eldman had lost his life. And Danny Bellino, who was found guilty of second-degree murder, would lose most of his youth and all of his innocence in prison. I felt sad for Danny. Despite the savagery of the crime, I still saw him as a decent person, perhaps more fragile than the rest of us, who had been pushed too hard for too long.

As I drove north, with the radio playing softly in the car, I thought a lot about Danny. I knew there weren't too many Danny Bellinos in my files. But there were a lot of Mark Eldmans. A "homicide concealment" is the professional term for someone who is missing because a murderer had hidden the body. The trouble was that I had no way of knowing which ones they were. And so I would go on looking for every person as if he were still alive, and hoping I was right.

By the time of Danny Bellino's trial in 1981, I was well established as a professional investigator. I was finding most of the people whom I looked for. I was getting assignments from insurance companies, and they were happy with my work. Newspaper reporters called me every month or so to write stories about missing-person work, and I appeared from time to time on television stations. Law-enforcement agencies from many parts of the country called me for advice on cases, and my mailbox usually contained a letter or two from a searching parent looking for encouragement and direction.

I looked forward to the day when I wouldn't have to bring up two boys in a small apartment in the city. Just the fact that I could soon make a down payment on a house seemed like a miracle to me. I was surviving on my own. I was taking care of my boys. I had a career and I was good at it.

So, Marilyn, I often asked myself, why do you feel like such a fraud?

11

In April of 1982 I was driving from New York City to Schenectady after working on a compensation case, when I decided to stop at New Paltz to visit the office of Child Find. Child Find was then a fledgling volunteer organization which had been formed to disseminate information about missing children, especially children who had been abducted by parents. I had called Child Find twice before, trying to get information about the organization, but each time, as soon as I mentioned that I was a private investigator, the voice on the phone had gone cold and the conversation had quickly ended.

The Child Find office was in small, cramped quarters on the lower floor of the town hall, the kind of place where nonprofit organizations usually find a home. Child Find was operating on a shoestring budget of donations and volunteer help.

I introduced myself to Gloria Yerkovich, the woman who had started Child Find. She was a slim, unusually attractive woman who eyed me suspiciously from behind the desk. I could see that she was not anxious to spend a lot of time chatting with me.

Gloria had poured her heart into Child Find. She told me that her own daughter was missing and the experience of trying to find her had left Gloria with a deep sense of frustration.

As we sat in her office talking, she was polite but somewhat guarded. I surmised that private investigators were not her favorite people.

"I admire what you're doing," I said at one point. "It takes a lot of energy and commitment to put in volunteer hours."

"Oh," she said, somewhat puzzled, "you know a lot about volunteer work, do you?"

"Oh, yes," I said, "I put in twelve years as a volunteer in search-and-rescue."

"Oh," she said. Now she leaned forward and looked at me more carefully. Her face softened and her lips rose in a friendly smile. It was as if, in the acknowledgment that we had both done volunteer work, we suddenly understood each other better.

"Look," she finally said, "I'll be frank with you. I don't know you, but I do know private investigators. They come in here all the time. They don't care about these kids. Very often their priority is the fee they ask of desperate parents."

"I understand," I said. It saddened me, but I couldn't honestly rush to the defense of my profession. Gloria was essentially telling the truth. Not all investigators are that way, but somehow the bad ones stand out, and that is what the public sees.

"I didn't come here to get cases," I told her. "I came here to see if you were a resource that I could recommend to my clients."

Gloria stared at me.

I stared at her.

"I'm looking for something a little more reliable than psychics," I said, and we both laughed. Then I told her my Roberta Garlandi story, and we laughed some more.

After we had talked for another fifteen minutes, I think Gloria was convinced that I was honest. I asked her if I could pull a couple of files and work on them. No charge.

I took the files home with me, and within a week I had found three kids for Child Find. The first was a girl named Anita Rudd who had been missing for eighteen years. She was a young woman living in California by the time I had found her, and when I phoned her mother, a lawyer, at work to tell her that her daughter had been located in San Francisco, I heard the phone drop to the floor and bounce. In the background I could hear crying and a muffled "oh, god, oh, god." I heard a woman's voice saying, "Mrs. Rudd, what's wrong? What is it, are you all right?" Mrs. Rudd's crying continued until someone picked up the phone. A man's voice said, "Hello, I don't know what you told Mrs. Rudd, but she's broken down completely. I'll have to have her call you back." I hung up knowing that the woman was crying tears of joy. When she called back ten minutes later, there was a tone of embarrassment in her voice. "I haven't cried in eighteen years," she said, "I didn't realize how much I'd held it in until you called."

"It's perfectly all right," I said.

"I kept an album for her," she said. "In it I put her birthday cards and my thoughts at Christmas. I didn't know where to send anything, so I kept an album in the hope that I would be able to give it to her someday. I want her to know that although I wasn't there for her first day at school, or to comfort her through the mumps, I wanted to be there. Now I have the chance to tell her that."

When Child Find moved to larger quarters, in a building across the parking lot from the original office, I was invited to the opening celebration. I sat beside a man who had been introduced to me as someone who had been "very helpful" to many organizations throughout the country. As we sat there drinking our punch, I looked across the room at all the people who had donated time, money, and energy to find missing kids.

"It's a great feeling to know we can do some good, isn't it?" I said.

"Don't be so naive," he replied. "I made a quarter of a million dollars my first year in the missing-children field."

The man was an investigator who was charging parents

large fees for finding kids, sometimes for doing no more than a motor-vehicle check or making a few phone calls. At the time, Child Find had no investigators of their own; they functioned strictly as a collector and distributor of information.

That conversation robbed me of some enthusiasm. I felt bad for all the dedicated people in that room who were donating funds and a part of their lives to the cause. Later, when Child Find asked me to be their first in-house investigator, I felt that my personal standards and values had been noticed and were desired.

For months, I spent most of my weekends in the Child Find office. Usually I would drive the one hundred miles to New Paltz, work all day and evening on the phone, at the typewriter, and reading files, until I fell into a light sleep on the leatherette love seat in Gloria's office. Sleeping on the love seat was about as comfortable as sleeping on a coffee table, but it was all that was available; and after a few weeks I knew enough to throw a blanket and a pillow in the car with me. I would wake up early, make myself some coffee, then work all day Sunday and drive home in the evening.

I handled hundreds of cases for Child Find, and most of them had happy endings. The organization grew to service all kinds of missing-persons cases. The color of the folders on my desk or in the files told me the type of disappearance. Yellow was for an adult disappearance. Blue was for a stranger abduction. Tan, the most common, was for a parental abduction. Some cases dragged on for months. Others were settled in a day. My fastest case involved a child who had been missing for over seven years.

I had come to the office on Wednesday to catch up on some work. I was eating lunch at my desk when Richard and Sal Rizzo came in. Richard Rizzo was about thirty-five. He was well dressed and had dark hair. The top buttons of his shirt were open and three or four gold chains flashed against his chest. With him was his father, Sal, a silver-haired man who nodded and smiled after everything that Richard said.

Richard had been divorced, and his wife, Donna, had gotten custody of their two-year-old son, Anthony. Richard called him "Tony." Though Richard had visitation rights, Donna had run away with the boy and Richard had not seen his son since 1975.

Like so many parents, Richard had assumed that if the police couldn't find Donna, then he certainly couldn't. The problem with that thinking, I explained, was that it assumed the police had searched diligently, which may not have been the case. The years rolled by, the Christmases without his boy, the summers, the birthdays, and Richard had gotten more and more distraught. He had checked in with the police now and then, but they never had anything to report. Then, when Richard and Sal had seen a Child Find poster in a coffee shop, they decided to drop in.

Richard grew increasingly agitated as he told me the story. He waved his hands and raised his voice.

"He gets like this when he talks about Tony," the grandfather explained. I could see that there were tears in Richard's eyes.

"I've never seen my boy walk," he said. "I've never heard him talk. It's not right."

"Did Donna ever have a life-insurance policy?" I asked, rolling a sheet of paper into the typewriter while Richard leaned on my desk.

"Yes," he said.

"What was her maiden name?"

"Donna Ascera," he said. "And sometimes she calls herself Elena. That's her middle name."

"When was she born?"

"December 29, 1951."

"Excuse me," I said. I walked across the room to a corner desk where there was a phone. The two men looked at me as if I had just abandoned them.

I called Dan Rochester, a friend who worked at an insurance company. Dan had access to a national insurance computer. I asked him to run Donna Rizzo's name through the computer. Nothing came up. Then we tried Donna Ascera, Elena Ascera, and Elena Rizzo. Still nothing.

I went back and talked to Richard and his father again.

"Did your wife go to college?" I asked.

"No. She was taking night courses at the state university when we split up. Those were the times when I got to be alone with Tony, and I was good with him, wasn't I, Papa?"

His father nodded.

"Excuse me," I said again, heading back toward the phone. Richard threw his hands in the air; he was frustrated because I kept interrupting his story.

I called the state university on a pretext. I told them that I was the personnel director at R. Joseph Paul and Company. Donna had applied for a position with us, I said, and I needed a copy of her transcript. I gave them a downtown address.

"But while I have you on the phone," I said, "I wonder if you could give me Donna's address. It seems to be smudged on the application."

"I'm sorry, but we can't give out that information over the phone."

Two strikes, I thought. I went back to the men. By now Richard Rizzo was so worked up that he was pacing across the office, unable to remain seated. His father understood Richard's frustration and tried to calm him down.

"She should not have done this," Richard said. "She had no right. I want my son. I have a right to see my son. He's my son. Papa, he's your grandson. She has no right, she has no right."

"It's okay, it's okay," the father was saying. "Mrs. Greene will try to help us."

"But she keeps going away," Richard said. "Every time I try to tell her something she walks away."

"Does Donna have a driver's license?" I asked. He stopped pacing long enough to answer me.

"No," he said. "I mean, she didn't have one seven years ago. Now, who knows?"

"Excuse me," I said. I went back across the room to the phone. Richard looked at his father and shook his head.

It was time to check out the registry of motor vehicles. The state department of motor vehicles had become one of my best sources of information. Sooner or later almost every adult gets a driver's license or registers an automobile. The state registries will provide motor-vehicle-registration information to anybody who fills out the proper form and mails it in with two dollars. I had spent many nights at my kitchen table filling out requests for motor-vehicle information, usually for a dozen or so states where I thought a person might be, but sometimes for all fifty. A response to one of these mailed-in requests usually took two months. However, since I made so many requests in New York, I had gotten a credit account with the department of motor vehicles. I could get information by phone, simply by telling them my account number, which was then billed two dollars for each name I ran through their computer.

It took me ten minutes to get a motor-vehicle clerk on the phone. I gave her my account number and asked her to try the name Donna Ascera, and I gave her the date of birth. The computer showed that no Donna Ascera with that birth date had a driver's license or motor-vehicle-registration in the state of New York. Then I tried Donna Rizzo. Same answer. Then Elena Ascera and Elena Rizzo. No luck. Either Donna had moved out of state or she had never gotten a driver's license. It was hard to imagine an unmarried woman with a small child getting by without a driver's license.

"Is that all?"

"Huh?"

It was the registry clerk. "Is that all?" she asked. "Do you want to try any more names?"

"No," I said, disappointed. And then something occurred to me. Perhaps it was my intuitive right brain putting in its two cents, since my logical left brain wasn't getting anywhere. "Wait," I said, "try Donna Elena."

It was a long shot, but maybe she liked both given names so much that she put them together.

A few seconds later the clerk came back on the phone. "I have a Donna Elena, born 12-29-51; address, 73 Rowe Street in Utica."

"That's great," I said, "just great," as I scribbled the information on a scrap of paper. I glanced across the room at Richard and his father. Richard was talking and pacing. His father was nodding.

I called telephone information and asked for Donna Elena at 73 Rowe Street in Utica.

"I'm sorry," the operator said, "I don't show any Elena at that address."

Then I went through the names all over again. Donna Rizzo. Elena Rizzo. Donna Ascera. Elena Ascera. While I waited for the operator to check on the names, I gave some thought to why I often felt like a fraud who was posing as a private investigator. It was, I supposed, because so much of what I did was not clever at all. It was things like this—making phone calls, filling out forms, watching someone's house. And yet, when it all worked and I came up with someone's child or wife or husband, people carried on as if I had performed a miracle. I felt embarrassed being credited with near miracles when all I had really done was common-sense legwork.

After I had tried all of Donna's names unsuccessfully, I decided to call information again and try Donna Elena. I was pretty sure that if Donna was using that name on her driver's license, she would go with that name for everything else. Maybe the operator just made a mistake.

I glanced over at Richard, who was unaware of what I was doing. He looked helpless. My heart fell. With him, as with all my clients, I feared that I wouldn't be able to help—that I wouldn't be good enough.

"I do show a Donna Elena at 128 Highland Avenue," the operator said. She gave me the number. I wrote it down.

I dialed the number and a little boy answered.

"Hi," I said, "is this Tony?"

"Yes."

"Is your mommy home?"

"Yes." The little boy put the phone down and I hung up. I took the piece of paper with the number and address on it and walked back to the table where the father and son were sitting.

"I just don't know why Donna is doing this," Richard was saying. "I just want to see my son. I'm not going to run away with him like she did."

I put the piece of paper on the desk in front of him. "Your son is at this address," I said clearly, during a moment of silence.

Sal Rizzo's eyes lit up, but Richard kept right on talking. "I just want to spend some time with my boy. I want to teach him things. I want to buy him presents. Is that so awful?"

I sat with folded arms, amazed that Richard Rizzo hadn't absorbed what I said.

"Richie, Richie, Mrs. Greene has found Tony!" the grandfather said as he tugged on Richard's arm.

"There are things only a father can do for his boy," Richard was saying, still oblivious to the fact that his search was over.

The grandfather leaned over and snatched up the piece of paper, as if I might suddenly decide to take it back.

"How did you do this?" Sal asked.

"It's a long story," I answered. "But do me a favor. Get a

lawyer first. Don't just go barging in there. She could get panicky and run away again."

"Yes, I see," he said, and then he put an arm around his son, who still hadn't comprehended what was going on.

"Tony is here," he said, waving the piece of paper in front of Richard as he led him to the door. "She has found our boy. Thank you, thank you. Seven years we have been looking and you have found him in an hour."

"Twenty minutes," I said, looking at my watch.

He smiled at me. "It's a miracle," he said. "A miracle."

Working for Child Find was not very different from working for private clients. I still had to deal, in many cases, with people, including searching parents, who were mentally unstable. The issue of missing children was getting a lot of publicity, which was very attractive to people who were desperate for attention.

I was involved with a promotion in which several newspapers were donating space to publicize missing children.

One of the first children we used to publicize the program was a girl whose mother had reported her missing. The girl's picture appeared in the newspaper. It turned out that her file was completely contrived. The picture was actually of the mother herself when she was a teenager.

I don't know why somebody at the office didn't catch it. On her report, the woman had noted that she had recently been released from a psychiatric center. And, even more absurd, she had written that she hadn't seen her daughter since the girl was six. The girl in the picture was seventeen. It wasn't exactly Watergate, but it was a minor scandal, and we all felt embarrassed.

I continued to handle cases on my own. I saved money for a house. The truth, I knew, was that I was neither a fraud nor a miracle worker; but there was a growing hysteria over missing children, and it brought reporters to my door.

One morning a reporter came over and spent an hour

interviewing me. Because his paper circulated in northeastern New York, he asked a lot of questions about the Gary Vale case. Gary was the boy who had fallen into the slate quarry. After the reporter left, I phoned Mrs. Vale at work to let her know her case might be mentioned in the article. She wasn't there, so I left a message. Two minutes later she called back. I asked how she was doing.

"Marilyn," she said, "you don't know what it's like to lose a child. It's like losing your right arm. You've lost a part of yourself. The feeling of pain never goes away. It's been four years, and I still think about him all the time. There is not a waking moment when Gary is not on my mind. My other boy, Alan, has been through eleven schools and ten psychiatrists. Marilyn, that poor boy has such incredible feelings of guilt because of all the times he yelled at Gary, 'I wish you were dead,' and slammed a bedroom door. That's normal sibling rivalry. That's how brothers sometimes talk to each other, but when one dies, all those words come back as guilt. And I feel guilty, too. If only I had picked Gary up at school with the car. If I only had done this, if only I had done that. I've had to talk about it for years, but it just doesn't get any better. The pain just doesn't go away.

"The day after my son was found, a state trooper came to my house. He had to get information for a final report. Marilyn, I attacked that man. I mean, I just kept hitting him and screaming, 'Why didn't you believe me, why didn't you believe me?' I knew it wouldn't have made any difference. Gary was already gone. But I was just so filled with rage over the loss of my son."

Mrs. Vale said that she had joined a support group made up of parents who had lost a child. It was called Compassionate Friends; they have chapters all over the country.

"People attend meetings for years," she said. "They just can't get past their grief. They try, they really try. One woman lost her daughter to polio in the late forties, and she still comes to talk about her sadness."

She mentioned one man who drove all the way from Syracuse every week because he had to talk about his missing son who had never returned from a camping trip. I knew the man.

"That's why I had to call you back right away," Mrs. Vale said. "I couldn't put it off until tomorrow. I had to know what you wanted right away."

Mrs. Vale said, "The need to talk about my loss is a compulsion. It drives friends away. They can't stand to listen to it anymore. They can't bear being so close to your pain all the time. The guilt destroys relationships. My marriage broke up over this. I blamed my husband, he blamed me. Then we tried to console each other and couldn't. It can destroy your whole life. I'm trying to put mine back together.

"Last week, Gary's brother said something at a Friends meeting that shocked me because it had so much feeling and insight in it. The woman who had been going to meetings for thirty years looked at Alan and asked how long his brother had been gone. Alan never looked up; he stared at the floor and said, 'Two days.' Everyone at the meeting knew exactly what he meant. After four years it still feels like we lost him only yesterday."

I hung up the phone. I was limp. Marilyn, I thought, you don't know anything. You're no expert. You find these people but you have no idea what it is all about. I felt empty. It seemed as if I had learned about my subject until I couldn't learn any more, and now suddenly a door had been thrown open, a door that showed me how little I really knew.

12

I couldn't believe what I was reading.

Here was a woman whose son had been kidnapped and the authorities had done nothing to help her.

Her name was Audrey Loughlin, and her story was contained in the case file in front of me. It was a night in 1984, and I was in the Child Find office all alone. I had been shuffling through the files, hoping to find a case that I could handle quickly by phone; but a blue file folder in the file drawer had drawn my attention, because blue meant "stranger abduction," and those cases were rare, even though the media were portraying them as rampant. I had pulled the file from the drawer and read it even more intently when I saw that it belonged to a woman from Cohoes, New York, not far from where I lived.

Audrey's six-year-old son, Chris, had been taken from her by a baby-sitter in Texas three years earlier. I studied the report late into the night, with my legs curled beneath me on the love seat. The file troubled me, so I took it home.

Two days later, Audrey Loughlin came to my home and I interviewed her. She was a slim woman, thirty-two years old, with long curly brown hair. She was an attractive woman, but the past three years had stolen the light from her eyes. The pain that surrounded her was almost tangible.

By this time I had bought a small, split-level house in Schenectady, with a backyard and a pool for the kids, and as Audrey sat in my living room and told me about the hard times in her life, memories of my own poverty came back. Like her, I had gone through a bad marriage, I had watched unpaid bills pile up, and I had experienced the frustration of trying to raise children in a small apartment.

Audrey asked about my children and, though I was supposed to be interviewing her, we ended up talking about my boys for a while. I appreciated it. In the hectic pace of building my career, I hadn't really taken much time just to sit with a friend and talk about family.

My father had died, I told her, and like the death of my mother years ago, the tragedy seemed to cut more deeply into Paul. The loss of his grandfather so soon after the divorce had pushed Paul further into a protective shell that had been growing around him for years. He often descended into sullen moods. He argued with me. He threw tantrums. He did everything except say that he was hurting.

Audrey offered words of encouragement, and I felt from her a sense of envy that I, at least, could be with my sons to help them deal with their problems. I had my troubles with Paul, but I had not come anywhere near Audrey's misery. I could barely imagine how tragic it would feel to have Paul or Joey suddenly taken from me. Overall, things were going well for me, and that made me all the more anxious to help Audrey. As the conversation shifted from my story to hers, her body sagged, as if hope had been drained from it. She was a broken woman. I remember thinking that I wanted to put her back together.

In 1981, hoping to get a fresh start in life, Audrey had moved from New York to Houston with Chris, then six years old. Audrey's small savings ran out quickly and she couldn't find a steady job. She worked part time as a waitress at a restaurant called The Calder, and she worked as a secretary one day at a time for a temporary service, but the jobs never paid her enough for food, rent, and day care for Chris.

Deborah Brown, a full-time employee at The Calder, offered to take care of Chris until Audrey could get on her feet. Deborah had three children of her own. She had taken care of Chris before and was extremely fond of the boy. Chris was a quiet kid who liked to play with toy planes and his collection of action figures. He would not be a problem. Deborah was not much better off than Audrey, but she did have an apartment, she was home during the day, and she seemed to be a warm and loving person who could give Chris the emotional nourishment he needed during these tough times.

After Chris had been with Deborah's family for two weeks, Audrey found an apartment and a job in another part of Houston. She called Chris every night. And then one night, when she was ready to bring her son back to live with her in her new home, Audrey called and got a telephone-company recording that said the line had been disconnected.

Audrey drove to the house. A neighbor told her that Deborah Brown had moved.

"But she couldn't have moved," Audrey told the neighbor. "She has my son. Where did she go?"

The neighbor told her that Deborah had left no forwarding address.

Audrey was in shock. It had to be some kind of crazy mistake. She went from house to house, asking other neighbors, but nobody knew where Deborah had gone. Audrey went to The Calder.

"Deborah hasn't shown up for work all week," she was told.

Two days went by. Three days. A week. And still no word from Deborah Brown.

When Audrey went to the Houston police, they told her that they couldn't accept a missing-person report because the child had been turned over to Mrs. Brown voluntarily. Audrey called the FBI. They said they could only become involved if it was a kidnapping, and that would require a ransom demand.

Audrey was also turned away by the Harris County District Attorney's Office.

"But my child has been abducted," she cried to the assistant D.A.

She was told that Chris's disappearance was not considered an abduction because there was no evidence that Mrs. Brown had left the state with Chris.

Inside Audrey there was a constant scream of frustration. Her son had been stolen from her and nobody seemed to care. Not one police authority at any level did anything to help her. She began to slip emotionally. She became a woman obsessed.

For the next year, Audrey worked during the day and spent her nights and weekends driving through the city looking for Mrs. Brown's pickup truck. She drove up and down the streets, she looked in driveways, she asked friends and strangers if they had seen her son or Mrs. Brown. She slipped deeper and deeper into depression. After a year of this, her family in New York, convinced that she was on the verge of a total breakdown, persuaded her to return for the moral support of her family. Audrey settled in Cohoes, but every time she saved enough money, she flew to Houston and resumed her search of the streets.

That day, when she spoke to me in the downstairs office of my Schenectady home, Audrey spoke quietly, but I could see that she was still screaming inside.

"Can you help me?" she asked.

I knew that finding Chris Loughlin would be a formidable task. He had been taken by someone named Brown. Why couldn't it be Kowalski, or Boggs, or even Henderson, I thought. Why did it have to be Brown? Many times over the coming months I would curse that name. The fact that Chris had been abducted by a woman added to the difficulty. In three years, Deborah might have gotten married and taken another name. On top of that, Houston was a town populated by out-of-staters. Deborah Brown could easily have been from Iowa, Oklahoma, Delaware, and she could just as easily have gone back. She could be anywhere. Chris was the needle and America was the haystack.

I began my search for Deborah Brown the same way that Audrey had. I called the police in Houston. They told me what they had told Audrey: They would not accept a missing-person report unless we could prove that the child had been taken out of Texas.

"But this woman took Mrs. Loughlin's little boy," I said. "Isn't that a crime?"

"How do we know it was her little boy?" was the reply.

I called the Texas State Police. They offered no help. I called the police in Cohoes. They wanted no part of it. I called the New York State Police. "An abduction in Texas is outside our legal jurisdiction," they said. They were right; they couldn't become involved. I called the FBI in Albany several times. Each time I called I spoke to a different person, and I had to explain all over again who I was and what had happened to Chris. One afternoon I could not bear to dance one more step in the bureaucratic shuffle.

I asked the agent on the phone, "To whom am I speaking?"

"I'm sorry, ma'am, I am not authorized to give you that information."

"What information? I'm just asking for your name so that the next time I call I can talk to you again instead of starting all over again with someone different, like I have three times now."

"Sorry," he said again, "I am not authorized to tell you my name."

"You can't tell me your name? I told you my name," I said. "I'm trying to find a little boy who's been missing for three years and you can't even tell me your name?"

"That's correct, ma'am."

"Is there some reason for that?" I asked.

"It's bureau policy, ma'am."

"What is the reason for the policy? I can't imagine how the public can communicate with their local FBI office if no one has a name."

The matter would have been funny if it hadn't been so serious.

"Well," he said, "we get a lot of calls from crackpots."

"I'm not a crackpot," I said. "I'm an investigator trying to find a missing boy."

"I'm sorry, ma'am, but I'm not allowed to give out the names of agents, including myself."

When I hung up, my hands were tense and half closed. I could only imagine what rage had burned in Audrey Loughlin since 1981.

Next I put in several calls to the Harris County, Texas, District Attorney's office, and still I got no closer to finding Chris Loughlin.

Then I wrote a long letter to the Texas Registry of Motor Vehicles, explaining the situation. Normally, you can't run a motor-vehicle check without giving the person's date of birth, but I had this idea that because a child had been taken from his mother, they might show compassion and print out a list of all the Deborah Browns for me. I was wrong. They turned me down. I wondered often what Chris was feeling and thinking.

As with all my cases, I kept careful records of who I talked to and what was said. On a Tuesday morning two weeks after I met Audrey Loughlin, I was alone in the Child Find office and I made what seemed like my one-hundredth phone call on the case. I called the police in Pasadena, which is a suburb of Houston.

"Sorry, ma'am, can't help you," he said.

He was polite. They were all so goddamn polite. I was angry. "Damn it," I said under my breath, "we have a child missing here and no one will help. No one. I can't believe it."

This period was at the beginning of the wave of publicity about missing children, and almost every day you could find a public official or law-enforcement officer discussing the issue on television. "We never turn down a missing-child case," they would say. "No amount of time or effort is too great to find a missing child." "Not true," I said, while shaking my head. "It's just not true."

I began to build a profile of Deborah Brown. I had to put together as many facts as possible. I brought Audrey to my house and I spoke with her for five hours.

"How tall is Deborah?" I asked.

"About five-foot-two."

"Are you sure?"

"I don't know. Something like that."

"Well, when you stood next to her, where was she on you?" Audrey put her hand against her body. I got a tape measure and checked it. "Five-foot, two-inches all right."

I cut pictures of women out of magazines. "Was Deborah's hair like this woman's? Or was it more like this one's?" I asked. "What about hair color? How much did she weigh? Did she wear any unusual jewelry, maybe a locket with somebody's name on it? Did you ever go to the beach together and take pictures?"

When I had wrung every bit of information that I could out of Audrey, I still didn't have much. Deborah Brown had blue eyes and blonde hair. She stood about five feet, two inches tall, and weighed about 220 pounds. She was about Audrey's age, which would probably put her birthdate somewhere between 1947 and 1951. I knew Deborah's old address, I knew she had worked at The Calder, and I knew the names of her children.

The weight was the best part. If I could find somebody who had met a 220-pound Deborah Brown, it would probably be the right Deborah Brown.

I began another series of phone calls. This time I called

Texas private detectives and asked them for professional favors. An investigator in Texas never knows when he might need some help from one in New York, so there was a lot of cooperation; but I didn't want to push my luck, so I didn't ask too much from any one investigator.

One investigator, Harry Evans, went to The Calder for me. He read the bar's employment records, but they were a mess. The lounge had changed hands and none of the paperwork concerning Deborah Brown had survived.

"But I did talk to one waitress who worked with Brown," he told me over the phone. "She doesn't know anything current about Brown, but she said she had seen her around for years before they worked together."

This was encouraging. I was beginning to feel sure that Brown was a native Texan.

Another private detective had a connection at the registry of motor vehicles. I couldn't ask him to pull every Deborah Brown in Texas out of the computer; professional courtesies go just so far. But I did ask him to run the first forty for me. The list did not carry birth dates, but it did include the addresses and the hair and eye coloring of all the Deborah Browns. Half of them were blue-eyed blondes.

With this information, I again started calling local police departments in the Houston area. I called six local police departments, told them about the missing kid, and asked them to run a few of my blue-eyed blonde Deborah Browns through their computers to see if they could find one who was born between 1947 and 1951.

I knew the police weren't allowed to give me the details, but I reasoned that anyone we ruled out could reduce the size of the haystack.

Just as each case has its elements of frustration, sooner or later each case doles out a little bit of luck. My luck came this time in the form of a police officer who had the habit of reading out loud.

He was at the seventh police station I called, and he

must have had the computer screen near the phone. I could hear the clunk as he put the phone down, and after a minute I heard him talking to himself. "Here's one," he said. "Deborah Brown. Blonde hair, blue eyes, date of birth—seven-thirteen-fifty." I wrote it down.

When he came back to the phone, he said, "Ma'am, I've got one, but I can't give the information over the phone. You'll have to get it requested by your local police department."

"I understand," I said. "Thank you."

It was still a long shot, but it was something. Now I had a Deborah Brown with the right hair and eye coloring, who had been born about the right time.

With a date of birth I could run a motor-vehicle check.

I had to do it by mail. It took six weeks for the Texas registry to get back to me with Deborah Brown's driving record. Though Chris had already been gone for three years, the six-week wait was still painful for Audrey. Each day since his disappearance had been a trial for her. Each day that Chris was gone was one more day of Deborah Brown being his mother and one less day of Audrey having her son in her life.

One Monday morning the mailbox in front of my lawn contained an envelope from the Texas Registry of Motor Vehicles, and I tore it open even before I walked back to the house. It contained the driving record of a Deborah Brown. Please let it be the right Deborah Brown, I prayed. With the morning breeze blowing through my hair and my heart pounding wildly, I read the report. This Deborah Brown had been stopped for speeding three years earlier. In Texas the police write the name of your employer on tickets. This Deborah Brown had told the police officer who ticketed her that her employer was The Calder Lounge.

"The Calder!" I shouted.

I was ecstatic.

The driver's-license information listed the old address,

which I already knew, but I didn't care. At least I knew I was working on the right Deborah Brown.

I called Audrey. "The haystack is shrinking," I said.

"What?"

"Look," I said, "I haven't found her yet, but I want you to know that the Deborah Brown I sent for is the right one. It's the Deborah Brown who took Chris."

For a long time I heard nothing except the sound of Audrey sobbing.

"Does this mean we're going to find Chris?" she cried. "Are we really going to find him?"

"We'll find him," I said. "I don't know where or when, but we'll find him."

Although driver's licenses were renewed only every four years in Texas, I knew that automobile registrations had to be renewed yearly. Now I had enough information to run a vehicle-registration check, which I hoped would provide me with a current address.

It did.

Deborah was living in a suburb of Houston. But the address was a post-office box.

At the Albany library I pulled out the Houston phone book. In my notebook I jotted the numbers of all the Deborah Browns and D. Browns with the proper exchanges. I knew that it was possible for Deborah to have a post-office box in one town, yet live in another, but my instincts told me that a woman who weighs 220 pounds doesn't travel any farther than she has to in order to pick up her mail.

My fourth call went to a Deborah Brown on Stapler Street. A woman answered the phone.

"Is this Deborah Brown?" I asked.

There was a pause.

"You have the wrong number," she said. She hung up.

I put down the phone. I had just spoken to the right Deborah Brown, I was sure of it, and my northern accent had probably alarmed her. But I had found her, there was no doubt in my mind. I could only hope that I wasn't about to lose her again, that she wasn't at this very moment packing and gathering the children, including Chris, for a trip to god knows where.

I immediately called the police in Texas and told them that I thought I knew the whereabouts of an abducted boy. They turned me over to the juvenile division, where I talked to Officer Doris Tennov.

Calmly and quietly I recited the whole frustrating series of events to Officer Tennov, which by now had become a litany of anguish. When I had finished my sad tale, Doris said, "Why, that's unconscionable."

"Finally!" I said.

"What?"

"Finally someone cares," I said. "You are the first person in Texas who has shown any sense of outrage over what happened to Audrey Loughlin."

"Tell me what Chris looks like," she said.

I described Chris as he looked the last time Audrey saw him, and I told her that he would now be nine years old.

"Look," she said, "it might take some time, and I might have to do it off duty, but I'll find out if a boy fitting that description lives in the house on Stapler Street."

Two weeks later my phone rang in the afternoon. It was Doris.

"The boy is there," she said.

"What do we need to do to pick him up?" I asked.

"The mother will have to go through the courts," she said. "She'll have to apply for custody."

"Of her own son?" I asked. It sounded insane.

"Yes. She can't just walk in and say some kid is her son. Where's the proof?"

Doris was right I thought. I hung up, knowing I was about to put Audrey through more emotional strain. I had to tell her that I had found her son but she couldn't have him back, yet.

Audrey Loughlin had been through three years of a mother's worst nightmare. She and I together had been through three months of searching. I didn't want to tell her where Chris was because I was afraid she would fly down to Texas and try to take Chris back. It could get ugly. Also, though I didn't say this to Audrey, there was a strong possibility that Chris would not want to come back. Deborah had been his mother for three years now. He was in school. He had friends. Would he want to leave all that he knew?

I made Audrey promise to go through the courts for custody. Then I gave her the address.

While the enormous amount of misguided publicity given to child abductions had done a lot of harm, in this case publicity did some good. Audrey had no money for lawyers, but the local newspapers and television stations were anxious to publicize her plight. We hired a lawyer and raised two thousand dollars in donations. After the lawyer got a writ of habeas corpus, the Texas police took Chris into protective custody. Incredibly, Deborah Brown also filed for custody.

On a bright autumn morning which we both hoped would be Audrey's last without her son, I drove Audrey Loughlin to the airport, where she got on a plane to Texas for the custody hearing. When I got home from the airport that day, I had a dozen or so cases I could work on, but my mind refused to focus. I glanced at the phone all day, as if looking at it would help it to ring. When it finally did ring, I pounced on it.

"Audrey?" I practically shouted.

"They're giving me my son back," she cried. "My baby."

The judge had awarded her custody. Deborah Brown, who had not been charged with any crime and never would be, would be allowed to see Chris one more time.

"I still haven't seen Chris," Audrey said. "They'll bring him to the courtroom this afternoon."

I was not anxious to puncture Audrey's bubble, but it was time for some counseling. I needed to prepare her for the worst.

"Audrey, be careful," I said. "Be understanding. Chris was six when you last saw him. He's nine now. Most of us don't remember much before the age of five, so that means he has spent most of his formative years with Deborah Brown as his mother. He probably calls her Mom."

"I know," she said. "Every time I think of that, I cry."

"He may love her very much," I said. "She has acted as his mother. She's taken care of him when he was sick. And she could have told him any number of things about you. Maybe she told Chris that you didn't want him anymore. Maybe she told him you're dead. When you see him, he may scream and cry. He may express hatred. He may say he doesn't want to be with you. He may kick you. He may bite you. This is a boy who is being taken away from everything that is familiar to him. Audrey, whatever you do, don't get mad at him. Just hug him. Just love him and understand the confusion he's feeling."

When I finished talking to her, there were tears in my eyes. I felt as if I were talking about my Paul.

It was late that night, after she had put her son to bed for the first time in three years, that Audrey called again from her Houston motel room to tell me what had happened.

"They put me into a big empty courtroom," she said, her voice still choked from the emotions of the day. "There were all these benches. I could smell the polish on them. It was the kind of room where you can hear your footsteps echo. And I just sat there all alone. I listened to the clock ticking. That's all I could do, listen to the clock ticking. I waited twenty minutes. Then, way down at the other end of the room, a door opened. It was a huge wooden door that went from floor to ceiling. Only Chris came through the door. Marilyn, my heart was beating a mile a minute. I'd been thinking about all the things you'd said. Maybe Chris would even hate me for letting this happen to him, I didn't know, but when he saw me his eyes lit up like they would just bug out of his head. Oh, Marilyn, he ran across the room crying 'Mommy,

Mommy.' He jumped into my arms and hugged me and kissed me, and he kept saying 'Mommy, Mommy, I tried to call you but I forgot the number—I wanted to come home and I didn't know how. I tried but I didn't know how.' "

When Audrey and Chris arrived in Albany, reporters from all the area papers were there to meet them, along with camera crews from the TV stations. We held a press conference at a small hotel. I was feeling elated for Audrey.

The child at the center of all this publicity, however, was not impressed. When the reporters were done asking me questions, I looked for Chris, and when I found him I leaned down and pressed my hands on his shoulders. He was an adorable little boy. Thinking about the three years of motherhood that had been taken from Audrey, I realized how lucky I was to have my sons at home. In that moment I resolved to do whatever it took to get through to Paul, to make him feel loved.

"How are you doing, Chris?" I asked.

"Okay," he said.

Then his mother said, "Chris, do you know who this woman is?"

"Nope," he said, and he squirmed away. Somewhat baffled by all the attention he was getting, he swung around quickly and bumped into a reporter. The reporter crouched down and put an arm around Chris. "So, young man," he asked, "how did you feel about being missing?"

Chris made a face, as if that were the silliest question he had ever been asked. "I wasn't missing," he said. "I was in Texas. My mother was missing, but I found her."

13

It was the end of a long day of helping the Seventy-Six Search and Rescue Team search for a man who had been missing eighteen days. Because 76–SAR didn't use air-scent dogs, they occasionally asked me to join them on a search. The missing man had walked away from a nearby adult home.

As I stood on a hill looking out at the scenery, I could hear below me the sounds of the other searchers working their way down to their cars. Just ahead of me, sitting on the ridge with his arms wrapped around his knees, was the man who had found the body. He was staring off at the horizon, perhaps thinking about the search and its outcome, as many of us often did.

I walked close behind him. When he heard me, he turned his head and looked up at me. "Kind of makes you think about your own mortality, doesn't it?" he said.

"Yes," I replied.

He leaned back, extended his hand. "Ed Van Wormer," he said. He was a stocky, bearded man. His hand was strong and darkly tanned like his face.

"Marilyn Greene," I said, shaking his hand.

"I know who you are," he said. "You get a lot of ink."

"Ink?"

"Publicity."

"Oh. Yes, I guess I do," I said, feeling, as I often did, embarrassed by that fact. "How come you're not with the others? They're all going for a drink."

"A drink?" he said. "I'll be lucky if I can eat breakfast tomorrow after seeing that guy."

"Your first search?"

"No," he said, "but it's the first time I found someone."

"You'll get..."

"What?"

"I was going to say you'll get used to it, but that's not true. You never really get used to it."

I sat beside him in the grass. "Feel like talking?" I asked.

"Sure. I just don't feel like leaving. It's so beautiful up here."

I asked Ed how he got into search-and-rescue work, and he told me that he had been in the civil air patrol and had gone on both ground and air searches. Later he joined the army and took law-enforcement courses to become a military policeman. He had never given much thought to the missing-person aspect of police work, he said. Even now, search-and-rescue was not his true love.

"What is?" I asked.

"Auto racing. I like to drive cars and I like to fix them. Of course, I love the water, too. I do a lot of scuba diving."

"I could have used you in Louisiana," I said, and I told him about the Spensers, who had probably driven off the bridge and into the water.

We spent a half-hour exchanging search stories, and then we worked our way down the mountain and said goodbye. I drove home thinking that he was nice and that I had enjoyed talking to him. I didn't expect to see him again.

A week later the phone rang and it was Ed. We swapped pleasantries for five minutes and then he finally got around to his reason for calling.

"Well, anyway," he said, "I thought, since we're both interested in S-and-R and since I enjoyed talking to you the other night, I thought, well, maybe we could get together. You know, have a cup of coffee or something."

"I'd like that," I said.

We made a date and then Ed said, "I think I ought to tell you, I am involved with someone."

"I understand," I said. "No problem."

I was smiling as I hung up the phone. It hadn't even occurred to me to think of him romantically. Still, I was flattered that it had occurred to him.

We met at a small, brightly lit coffee shop about halfway between Ed's house and mine. I wore a skirt and blouse. Ed wore a jacket. We both looked a lot better than we had after the search.

"What's the matter?" he asked after he ordered coffee. We sat in a booth by a window.

I was feeling sad, but I had no idea it showed. Either I wasn't good at hiding my mood or Ed was good at spotting it.

"My son," I said. "Paul. We just got back from counseling."

"Feel like talking?" he said with a smile, mimicking the way I had said it to him on top of the mountain.

This was a troubled time in my life. I had come home twice and caught Paul, now thirteen, drinking. We had fought. I had pleaded with him to open up, but all he could say was, "You wouldn't understand." Now Paul and I were going to counseling every Wednesday afternoon, but we hadn't made any progress. Paul was as impenetrable as a stone wall.

I hadn't intended to unload all of this on Ed, but I was frustrated and Ed was easy to talk to. For twenty minutes I sat across from him, dropping my problems on the table like so many parts of a broken machine.

"So everybody has problems," I said, when I had worn thin the subject of my teenaged son. "That's mine. Can you fix it?"

Ed shook his head. "No can do, ma'am. If it was a car I could fix it. Kids are not my speciality. I'll tell you one thing, though, when I was a teenager I was a little bit wild, too, and I've turned out okay. He'll be all right."

"Thanks," I said, though I wasn't so sure. "Anyhow, you've already helped just by letting me talk about it. That's what I really needed."

"Glad to be of service."

Ed asked about my work. I wasn't surprised; I had always found that people were fascinated by disappearances. But this was different. He listened with intensity. He asked what I did and how I did it, but he went deeper. He wanted to know why I did it, how I felt about it. He asked questions that no one had ever asked before.

I told him about the dogs and the search teams and the tendencies of missing people. I told him about the public records I used, the cases I'd been on, the desperate parents and husbands and wives, the clues, the hunches, the reports, the files. Ed was fascinated by even the most mundane details of my daily work.

"Sounds as if you really love your work," he said. He glanced at his watch. We had been talking for an hour and our coffee cups had been refilled three times.

"I do," I said, "but, you know, what I do sometimes seems so simple that I feel like a fraud." He was the first person I had ever said that to.

Ed grinned. "Well, of course you do," he said.

"Huh?"

"Everybody does," he said, "everybody who's really good at what they do."

"I don't understand."

"The better you are at something, the simpler it seems."

"I suppose, but..."

"Look," he said, leaning closer, "when I was a kid and didn't know a thing about auto mechanics, I went looking for a job in a garage. A guy says to me, 'Hey kid, you want a job, huh? Let me see you take the rear end out of that Chevy.' The truth is, I couldn't tell the rear end of a Chevy from a turnip. But I played it cool; I got under the car and acted as if I knew what I was doing. It took time, but I figured it out; I got that rear end out. The guy was impressed with me and he gave me my first job as a mechanic. And I was impressed with myself. I thought I was pretty clever. I was impressed with myself because auto mechanics still seemed complicated to me. Now, when I work on a race car and people are impressed, I don't understand it. It's all so simple to me that I don't see what the big deal is. That's because I know my field so well. I'm sure a brain surgeon feels the same way. Everybody's walking around telling him what a great surgeon he is, and he's thinking, 'Gee, it's just a frontal lobotomy, what's the big deal?'"

Ed smiled again. He looked at his watch once more and swallowed the last of his coffee. It was time to go. "I'll tell you what I think, lady," he said. "I think you really know your shit."

I couldn't recall getting such a descriptive compliment before.

Before we parted we made arrangements to meet again. It became a regular thing. Once a week we would meet for coffee. Usually we would begin with personal matters. I talked about Paul. Ed talked about his relationship with his girlfriend, which seemed to be unraveling. But before long we would be discussing things like runaways, abductions, homicide concealments, police departments, surveillance techniques, and underwater equipment that could be used on searches. I suppose our conversations made for some interesting eavesdropping at other booths, but we loved it. As Ed and I became better friends, he grew more and more interested in the field of missing persons. I told him that if I ever needed someone to help me with surveillance, I'd give him a call.

In April of 1985, I got a call from Terry Clifford in Kentucky. His son, Terry, Jr., had disappeared one afternoon on his way home from school. His parents, believing that the boy had been abducted, had put up a fifteen-thousand-dollar reward. While I could understand his desperation, I had to tell Mr. Clifford that fifteen thousand dollars was more than enough to lure every con man and shakedown artist east of the Mississippi. Mr. Clifford refused to withdraw the reward, but he wanted to hire me. He asked me to come to Kentucky.

A few days later, when I was making arrangements for someone to watch my boys while I was in Kentucky, Mr. Clifford called me.

"You don't have to come down here," he said. "Terry's in New York City."

He told me that he and his wife had gotten a letter from a Margaret Weaver in Oregon, and she had told them that Terry, Jr., could be found in New York City in a big brick building with black iron shutters and black shades. The building, they were told, was in the Bronx near the intersection of One Hundred Forty-ninth Street and Jackson Avenue, near St. Mary's Park. To the left of it there would be a guest house with three rooms, where Terry and other boys were being held prisoner.

"Miss Weaver says that if an investigator watches the building for a while, he'll see Terry come and go freely," Clifford told me. He asked me to find the place and get his son.

I was, understandably, interested in where Margaret Weaver was getting her information, so I called her in Oregon.

She told me that she was the spokeswoman for a woman who was a medium—a person, she said, "of great spirit guidance, who works on missing-person and criminal cases all the time." The medium was connected to something called the Church of Divine Guidance. Miss Weaver said the medium had told her that Terry had been baited by pornographers.

"The man who baited him told him he would make more money than he ever dreamed of," she said. "So the boy went willingly. The man said he knew Terry would be a hard worker."

She described the building and the guest house to me,

just as she had to the Cliffords in her letter, and she said that a man named Frederico was somehow connected to the boy, but she didn't know Frederico's role.

"He could be the ringleader," she said ominously.

I asked Margaret if she had ever been to New York. She said she had not.

When I asked her how the medium worked, she explained to me that there are records that we build every day of our lives, "every moment that we live," she said. "These are God's judgment books."

"And the medium has God's permission to read them?" I asked.

"Exactly," she said. "She has pulled Terry's records and read them to find out what has happened to that poor boy."

Toward the end of our conversation, Margaret asked me to refer missing-persons cases to her, and she told me that she would pass them on to the medium for solution.

"I've got one for you now," I said.

While she waited on the phone, I went to my file cabinet and pulled out the file on Randy Scott, a closed case in which I had already found the boy. I was interested to see if that information had found its way into God's judgment books. I gave Margaret the name, birth date, and the date and place of the disappearance.

"Do these people have any money?" she asked.

"Not much," I said.

"Well, would they be willing to make a donation to the Church of Divine Guidance in return for the services of the medium if they are guaranteed results?"

"I'm sure they would," I said.

"Is there a reward?" she asked.

I told her no.

"Such a pity," she said. "Marilyn, I can't tell you how many people have promised donations and then forgotten about the medium when their loved ones were found."

She hinted broadly that the medium was having a hard time keeping up with the bills, but she did say she would pass the information along and we could discuss the amount of the donation later. She also confided to me that she hoped to become a private investigator some day.

I called the Cliffords and told them about my conversation with Margaret Weaver. I had already warned them that offering a large reward would cause them to be plagued by false leads and treacherous informants who would only muddy the waters. I thought this just proved my point, but they disagreed. They still wanted me to conduct a surveillance on the building in The Bronx.

"Okay," I said. "But I have to tell you, I am not optimistic."

My Roberta Garlandi experience had not been my last encounter with the world of psychics. During the intervening years I had found that the general public thought missing people were found as often by psychics as by private investigators. Almost without exception, the parents with whom I had dealt had at some point turned to a psychic to find their missing child. I knew it was futile, but it was easy to understand. When your child is missing you'll try anything.

I had found over the years that the psychics had no proven record of success. Some were sincere. Others were crooks. In many cases, I had found that a psychic had said to a parent something like, "I see your daughter, Emily. She calls to me. She's near a small house. I'm getting *green.* There are trees in the area." This is a description which applies to virtually every spot in the country, with the exception of Death Valley and parts of eastern New Jersey. Sometimes, when the missing person had been found half a mile from a small house with two maple trees in the yard, the psychic had filed a claim for the reward money, saying he or she had given crucial information.

While I placed no value on the visions of psychics, I was

willing to check out a lead if my client still insisted, after I had counseled against it.

I called the New York City Police to see if the building Margaret Weaver had described really existed. They told me that a six-story apartment building with iron bars on the windows was located across the street from St. Mary's Park, but they didn't know about any guest house.

Then I called Ed.

"Do you still want to do a surveillance?" I asked.

"Sure."

"Well, here's your chance. I want you to go to The Bronx and check out a lead on the Terry Clifford case."

"Great!"

"Well," I said, "you might not think it's so great when I tell you where the lead came from. A psychic in Oregon. She read about it in God's judgment books."

There was a long silence. And then, "Oh."

"Still want to go?" I asked.

"Sure," Ed said. "Besides, who knows, maybe the psychic will turn out to be right."

Ed spent two days parked in a camper van across the street from the Bronx building. He photographed everybody who went in or out. Toward the end of the second day he started asking questions. There was no sign of Terry, no hint of a pornography ring, and nobody who had ever heard of Frederico. We never found Terry Clifford. But when Ed was done, he came to my house, turned in his film, and described the two tedious days as if they had been an adventure. "It wasn't so bad," he said. He was actually smiling. He had put in two long days at the most boring part of my profession and he was still enthusiastic. This was my kind of guy. I knew that we would work together again.

By this time Ed had broken up with his girl friend. As Christmas approached that year, we gradually revealed to each other our loneliness. I had my kids, Ed had his friends, but we each craved something more. We were both hurting from past relationships, and neither of us was in any rush to start something new.

On Christmas Eve, Ed showed up loaded down with presents for all his friends and family. Ed and I, along with Paul and Joey, spent the evening wrapping presents and listening to Christmas carols. Ed entertained the boys, Paul especially, with hot-rod stories and some of his sailing adventures.

"Some day I'll build a submersible so your mother can look for things underwater," he said.

"Really?" Paul asked. His eyes widened. "Can I help?"

"Sure."

Seeing this enthusiasm from Paul filled me with hope. Too much of his time lately had been spent staring mindlessly at the TV, and I had not been able to get him interested in my work. As I watched Ed and the boys, it saddened me to think there were men like Ed who would make good fathers but had no children, and kids like Paul who had never really had a father.

When the kids went upstairs to pretend they were sleeping, I pulled from the closet the gifts that I had bought for them. I had spent more than I could afford, but it was the season for that. Ed and I toasted the season with eggnog and rum. We sat near the Christmas tree and talked about our friendship, about rescues we had gone on together, and about the ways we could work together in the future. And there was a moment there, one I hadn't known in years, when our hands touched and we looked into each other's eyes like a couple of characters from a romance novel, and we knew that in our own way we were falling in love.

In the weeks that followed my connection to Ed grew stronger.

I continued to sleep in the Child Find office on weekends. And when I got home on Sunday nights Ed would be there for me.

"How many kids did you find this weekend?" he would ask.

"Three," I would say. Then he would pull out a bottle of champagne, which he hid in a different place every week, and I would tell him about the cases over a quiet dinner.

But the sad truth was that while my love affair with Ed was blossoming, my relationship with all the missing-children organizations was wilting. The missing-person field was being tainted by greed, and though Child Find maintained its integrity, it could not escape the pressure that the trendiness of the "missing-children issue" was putting on it.

More and more I was learning that my weekends at Child Find were resented by other investigators who felt I was closing cases that could have paid them large fees.

In time, the New York Attorney General's office investigated the relationship between Child Find, private investigators, and the parents of missing children. Some serious but false charges had been made. Over the course of six months, records were reviewed, investigators were subpoenaed, and charges flew. I was never touched by any of it. I wasn't even asked to testify. But the politics of missing children and the infighting among similar organizations saddened me. Something had gone terribly wrong in the missing-person field. Suddenly, looking for missing kids had become big business, and the money involved was bringing out the worst in people. It seemed as if the missing-children agencies were now placing a higher priority on fund raising than on finding missing children.

After the dust settled on the investigation, even though Child Find had been absolved of wrongdoing, the organization wasn't the same. Everyone was overworked and tired.

High salaries for fund raisers and administrators were being handed out at some of the nonprofit agencies.

Some were exposed by the media when it was found that little money was actually being spent on missing children.

One woman I spoke to at a conference made no bones about it: "Don't talk to me about dedication," she said, "I'm here because the board met my salary demand."

It appeared that my concept of participating in a project because of its humanitarian goals had become sadly obsolete. The national trend was to manage the missing-children agencies like businesses. So one Sunday afternoon I cleared out my desk, said goodbye to the love seat I had slept on so many times, and went home.

The following night, still stung by the sadness of what had happened, I sat alone at my kitchen table rereading the file of an unsolved case to take my mind off the fact that something was ending in my life.

Ed came in. He was drenched, but he was glowing with excitement. By this time, we had been working together pretty regularly. He grinned at me. Obviously, he had a story to tell, but he was going to make me wait.

"You're not going to believe this one," he said. He unloaded his camera equipment on the table and started rummaging through the kitchen cupboards for something to eat. He grabbed some crackers and sat down to tell me his story.

One of my insurance-company clients had hired me to check on an ex–prison guard who claimed he had severely injured his back during an inmate riot, and had left the force to stay home and live off a compensation check. The guard's father owned an auto-repair shop in a rural town, and the company had reason to believe that he wasn't so seriously injured that he couldn't work at his Dad's shop doing auto repairs and heavy labor. I had turned the case over to Ed for surveillance.

"So, anyway, I went there and I did the site evaluation," Ed said. Then he smiled and laughed at himself. "Jesus, I'm starting to use jargon. I mean I looked the place over. There was a long driveway and I couldn't very well stand there all day, so I looked around for a place to park where I could observe the shop from a discreet distance. There was a spot on a nearby road with a place where you could pull off and park. It overlooked the shop because it was up on the hill, and the view to the inside work bays was unobstructed."

"What time did you get there?" I asked.

"At eight o'clock, because I needed time to set up the camera equipment."

"So, what happened?" I asked.

"At nine o'clock the ex-guard shows up with his father. This seriously injured man did tune-ups on two cars; he did outside welding work on a large truck. Then he changed shock absorbers and unloaded a delivery of tires from a truck. He did everything but try out for the Olympics. Marilyn, you should have seen this guy, he was sliding between vehicles like a race-car driver. My back should be in such good shape."

"Great," I said.

"Not so great," Ed said. "There's more."

"Oh."

"At one o'clock the guy goes to lunch, and I probably should have left then. But I figured, what the hell, I might as well stay to see what his afternoon activities would consist of. At two o'clock I'm sitting there and my subject comes up from behind my vehicle, and guess what he has in his hand?"

"I don't know, what?" I replied with concern.

"A three-fifty-seven magnum handgun. Not a friendly gesture. Now, I'm fairly intelligent, and I had figured that the worst that could happen on this case was that the guy could come at me with a wrench or something and maybe brutalize the cameras. But this son of a bitch comes at me with a magnum the size of a Buick and he fires it into the ground."

"No," I said, "so what happened?"

"He forced me to empty the film from my cameras,

then he took me at gunpoint into the garage. I identified myself as an insurance investigator as he patted me down. He kept the gun pointed at me, even though he knew I was unarmed. He asked, 'How long have you been out there?' with a nervous tone to his voice. 'Long enough,' I told him. 'Got any more film?' he asked, pushing the gun forward toward me. 'No,' I replied.

"He paced back and forth in the garage for a while, then he went to the phone and called the police. Good, I thought.

"When the state trooper arrived, he looked at the ex–prison guard and said, 'Hi Jed, what have you got here?' Oh, God, I thought, these guys are buddies. What am I supposed to do, tell the trooper that his friend has committed an armed robbery by taking my camera and film at gunpoint?

"After the two of them spoke in a corner, the trooper searched me again, but he wasn't very thorough."

"No?"

"No," Ed said, sticking two fingers into the pocket of his shirt. He pulled out two rolls of film. "He missed these," Ed said.

Ed stared at me. "Marilyn," he said, "you're smiling. Here I am telling you this tale of danger and you have a smile on your face. I was sure you were going to be angry because I was spotted."

As he said it, I realized he was right. I was smiling. "You really love it, don't you?" I said.

"What?"

"Detective work. You really enjoy the challenge of conducting investigations, finding out the truth, bringing a missing child home, all that?" I said.

"Yes, I do," he said, "and I know that you do too!"

"Yes," I said.

We looked into each other's eyes, and without words we communicated that we would soon be sharing much more than just our careers. We married a short time after that.

14

When I had arrived in New Hampshire I'd found a note from Paul in my suitcase. I was surprised and curious.

"Dear Mom, when you get back on Friday can we have a date? Can we go out to dinner and go to a movie? Anything you want to see is fine. But just you and me, okay?"

The note brought tears to my eyes. It was so sweet, and yet so sad, that Paul didn't feel confident enough just to come out and ask me. I called him that night and promised that I would be home in time for our date.

Late on Friday, as I guided my car along the last few miles of the Massachusetts Turnpike toward the New York State line, the rain that had been falling all afternoon grew heavier and I worried about keeping that promise. I had spent three days in New Hampshire interviewing the parents and friends of a girl who had disappeared six years ago when she was fifteen. At one o'clock I had finished my last interview. Then the sky had turned dark and I knew the rain would slow my progress home.

It was 1986. For three days I had thought of nothing but the missing girl. Where had she gone and why? But it was as if the thoughts came in on the same frequency as the thoughts of my own troubled teenager.

Ed's presence in my life had inflamed the problems with Paul. It seemed that more than ever my older son felt unloved. Perhaps he saw Ed as his replacement. Or perhaps he saw Ed as one more person who would eventually abandon him. I didn't know. Paul didn't talk about it. But I did know that Paul had been drinking a lot, skipping school, and throwing tantrums. In his own explosive way, he was crying out for the world to notice him. Ed and I were running out of patience. Sometimes I felt like giving up on Paul, but I knew that this was mostly my own desperation when things were at a low point. But there were the other times, like this, when I thought, if I just spend more time with him everything will be all right.

At five-thirty I pulled into my driveway, thinking Paul and I would still have time to eat and catch a seven o'clock movie.

The boys were there to meet me at the door, staring anxiously out at the rain as I dashed from the car. Joey threw his arms around me and melted in my arms. Paul hugged me in the more reserved, slightly stiff manner that seems to be the style of boys when they reach a certain age. Then Ed gave me the warm hug I craved, but I could tell from the feel of him that something was wrong.

"Paul?" I asked.

"No. We had our usual problems, but that's not it. You've got company."

"Company?"

"Clients," he said. "They're downstairs."

"Oh, Ed, I can't. I promised Paul we'd go out."

"I know. I told them they could make an appointment, but they wanted to wait. Their son is missing."

I glanced at Paul, who was sitting in the living room, pretending that he didn't know what was going on.

"I haven't forgotten our date, honey," I called to him. "Just give me a few minutes."

"That's okay," he said. "I don't mind if we don't go out."

"No, it's not okay," I said. "We made a date and we're going to keep it. I've got to talk to these people right now; meanwhile, you decide where you want to eat and choose the movie, so long as it's not too scary."

I followed Ed downstairs. "Marilyn," he said, somewhat apologetically, "this is Mr. and Mrs. Parker." The Parkers, middle-aged and somber-looking, sat on the couch next to the office where Ed and I did most of our work.

Weary from my trip, I glanced around. Newspapers were scattered about. Dust had built up on the coffee table. The floor was decorated with a few odd-looking items that had been chewed beyond recognition by my dogs. There was a new gash in one of the wall panels, and I knew that Paul had probably thrown something in anger. And here were these two strangers looking very much like a church committee. I was embarrassed.

A moment later that seemed absurd. These people have a missing son, Marilyn, don't be a jerk. The dust on your coffee table is probably not high on their list of concerns.

I sat down on a hassock to face the Parkers and took my first look at them. What I saw shocked me. Don Parker was about fifty, portly but well groomed and well dressed. He had silver hair and sported a mustache. Eulla, his wife, appeared to be several years younger and had long brown hair, which she wore in a single loose braid down the middle of her back. To my surprise, it appeared as if she had not bathed in a very long time. The dirt on her thin arms was so conspicuous that it drew my attention, as did the smudge on her face that stretched from her chin to behind her ears. She wore an unadorned pink housedress that also looked old and soiled. On her lap was a large manila envelope, which she turned over and over in her hands as if she could make it into something better than it was.

Surprisingly, when Mrs. Parker spoke, the voice was that of a cultured and well-educated woman. She was articulate and had an impressive vocabulary and decorum.

I was certain the unwashed condition that was so apparent had been there long before her son had disappeared. I wondered if it had anything to do with his disappearance.

"We got your name from *Reader's Digest,*" she explained.

"They said you might be able to help." And then she told me about their son.

Peter Parker was a fourteen-year-old high-school freshman. One night after supper, Mrs. Parker had sent him out to the garage to take the household trash to the curb, but he never came back.

"It doesn't make sense," she said. "He finished eating supper at 6:05 P.M. and everything was fine. It was 6:20 P.M. when I sent him out with the garbage and he seemed okay. Peter liked doing his chores. At 6:35 P.M. I heard the garage door close. I waited a few minutes, and when he didn't come back inside the house I went out to see if anything was wrong. Peter was gone, so I went to the police station and reported him missing."

"As soon as you noticed he was gone you went straight to the police?" I asked.

"Well, of course," she replied.

"Did you feel that Peter might have gone to a friend's house?"

"No."

"Or that he might have walked to the store?"

"Oh, no," she said, "Peter wouldn't do that."

Mrs. Parker accounted for Peter's time with the precision of an accountant. She never said, "sometime in the afternoon"; it was always 2:10 P.M. exactly.

It had been a month since Peter disappeared. When I asked the Parkers what they had done in the meantime, they told me they had hired a private investigator named Rocco Faringay. I had heard of Mr. Faringay for years. He lived in Connecticut, as did the Parkers. He represented all that I found reprehensible about private detectives.

Faringay had come to the Parkers' house and offered to conduct an investigation for three thousand dollars. The Parkers agreed. Mr. Faringay searched the woods in the Parkers' neighborhood for a couple of days, then came back, said he had found nothing and had used up the fee. He wanted more money. Mr. Parker decided he was incompetent and forbade any more involvement with Mr. Faringay.

Two days later, when Mr. Parker was at work, Mr. Faringay returned and told Mrs. Parker that he could definitely find Peter, but it would require a more expensive investigation. He said it would cost thirty-five thousand dollars more. That was exactly what the Parkers had in their savings account. I suspected that Mr. Faringay had done an illegal bank check, probably through a friend. Mr. Faringay showed Eulla Parker how to liquidate the account in cash increments of five thousand dollars over several days' time. He knew that at ten thousand dollars the banks report the transaction to the IRS, and then there is a record of it. Mrs. Parker, confused and frightened by her situation, and possibly unstable to begin with, went along with it, believing it was the only way to get her son back. I am amazed at how some people show a complete lack of conscience when dealing with a vulnerable individual. Asking Mrs. Parker to pay thirty-five thousand dollars was like telling an elderly homeowner that his roof was going to fall in if he didn't pay you to repair it.

By this time, Mrs. Parker had found out that Peter took three hundred dollars from the house money and had taken a bus to Florida. A co-worker of Mr. Parker's had seen Peter at the bus station and told the family of it when word got out that Peter was missing.

"Is that the report?" I asked, glancing at the envelope in Mrs. Parker's lap. Don Parker had not spoken at all, but when Eulla had talked about liquidating the family's assets, he had slipped his arm around her in a gesture of emotional support.

She handed me the report.

Mr. Faringay said he had visited all the major tourist attractions in Florida, checking personnel records for Peter. He also had a list of names of people with whom he had spoken at numerous police departments and missing-children organizations. But there wasn't a word about what any of these people had said.

Although it wasn't in the report, Mr. Faringay had also told the Parkers that he had spent a week at a mercenary training camp in nearby rural Georgia. The camp was checked, according to Faringay, because a friend of Peter's had reported that Peter always wanted to be a mercenary, as he felt the life would be exciting. When the Parkers asked for the name and location of the camp, Mr. Faringay refused to give it, explaining that "these are very dangerous people, and we can't have you going there."

So what could I do? The Parkers were desperate and broke. I agreed to take their case for a small fee, which they would send in installments. They went home to Connecticut as a light rain began to fall. As I walked them to their car, I was concerned and wondered if bringing Peter home was really for the best.

"What could happen?" Paul asked me later at dinner. We had gone to El Camino, his favorite restaurant in Albany. I was surprised that we had fallen into a conversation about the Parker case.

"Well," I said, "judging from my interview with the Parkers, I would say that Peter had an unusual home life to deal with. The way his mother kept tabs on him, he probably felt trapped. Running away might have been his way of saying that he needs to experience self-direction."

"So what could happen if you brought him back?"

"Running away is sometimes an alternative to suicide," I said. "It's not always a good idea to take that alternative away."

"Oh," Paul said. And then, "What would you do if I ran away?"

"I'd find you," I said.

The subject changed after that. I asked Paul how he had gotten along with Ed while I was away. Paul grumbled and told me, as he had many times, that he disliked

Ed and wished he would leave. Though Paul had hit it off with Ed at first, the relationship had deteriorated as Paul began to realize how important Ed was in my life. Now he and Ed didn't even talk unless they had to, and Paul had developed the annoying habit of walking out of any room as soon as Ed walked into it. Ed had tried to build the relationship with Paul, hoping to give him the kind of male companionship he had never had, but Paul had slammed the door, literally as well as figuratively, in Ed's face. This, I knew, was a typical stepson–stepfather conflict. I had seen it in other families. I prayed that things would get better, but they never seemed to.

Lately, I had found that talking to Paul was like walking through a mine field. One moment he would be such a personable teenager—bright, witty, thoughtful. But he was also so fragile that one word, even the wrong tone, could sound to him like an accusation and send him into a defensive argument. He never poked his head too far out of the shell he'd been building around himself.

And so, sitting across from him in the restaurant, I chose my subjects carefully. I didn't bring up his grades. Paul was a bright student who was doing terribly in school. I didn't bring up the new gash I had seen in the wall downstairs. I didn't bring up the drinking. I wanted a pleasant, peaceful evening with my boy.

So we talked about the dogs. I still had Kili, and Ed had a young German shepherd that he was training for scent work.

"Hey, I know how we can make some big money," Paul said. "I've trained Kili to shag golf balls."

"Golf balls?" I asked.

"Yeah, you know how I like to putt golf balls in the yard? Well, Kili goes and gets them for me. It's great. It's like having my own caddy."

"And you're going to make money from this?" I laughed. It was great to see Paul enthusiastic.

"Mom, do you have any idea how many people putt golf balls in their backyard? Millions."

"I see," I said. "And we'll just rent Kili out to them."

"I thought of that," Paul said, "but it's not good business."

"No?"

"Kili can only be one place at a time," Paul said. "I've got a better idea. You and I will go around to people's houses and we'll train their dogs to shag golf balls. We'll make a fortune," he said, not really being serious.

After that we talked about sports, movies, television shows. We played guessing games, as we had when Paul was younger. There were moments when my mind wandered to thoughts of Peter Parker. But mostly I just listened to the music of my Paul's voice. It was wonderful to be able to just sit and relax with a glass of wine after dinner and stare into the face of my son without one of us yelling at the other. He's turning into a good-looking young man, I thought, and everything is going to be all right.

After dinner I glanced at my watch.

"Getting kind of late for a movie," I said. I thought he would be upset.

"That's okay," he said. "We can just sit and talk.

"What made you and my father break up?" he calmly asked.

I knew that Paul desperately needed the love of his father, who hadn't come to see him more than a dozen times in his whole life.

In the years since my first marriage, I'd had very little contact with Brad. His life had been hard, and the emotional problems caused by the war had made it difficult for him to hold a job. I knew he loved Paul, but Brad was never able to work through his own problems. It was probably better that he didn't visit during those times, but recently he seemed to be getting himself straightened out.

He had a new wife and a new job, and through years of therapy he had gotten control of his temper. I had hopes that he would establish something solid with Paul, but I knew that a lot of damage had already been done.

"Paul, do you remember the day your father and I broke up?" I asked. Paul was leaning back against his chair, his arms folded in front of him like a shield.

"No."

"You were just a baby," I said. "We were in the car, the three of us. You were sitting on my lap. Your father was driving. He had been very mixed up since coming back from the war, and I was getting afraid of him. I thought he would hurt us. We came to a street where there were four children playing ball in the middle of the road ahead of us—but I couldn't feel the car slowing down. I turned to your father and his eyes were like ice. He had an intense look, as if he were going to do something horrible. 'Brad,' I cried, 'slow down.' But it was as if I weren't even there. He aimed right for the children and jammed his foot on the accelerator. I couldn't believe what was happening. I shouted at him, 'Don't! Don't!' He kept going. So I pulled one arm tight around you and I leaned over and punched the horn so the kids would run away."

"Did they?" Paul asked, as if he dreaded the answer.

"Yes. They scattered just in time. You started crying something awful. You were so frightened. Your father just laughed it off, like it was all a joke. Then a little while later we stopped at a red light and things were very tense. Your father pounded on the steering wheel. It was as if something were pumping him up with pressure and it had to come out somewhere. He started hitting the steering wheel as if he were giving it a beating. You started crying again, which made Brad even angrier.

"Until then he had only punched objects; he had never hit you or me. But he had gotten more aggressive, and I knew it was just a matter of time before he would hit me. I had always told myself, 'Marilyn, if he hits you or Paul, hit him back.' So as I sat there at the traffic light with all this tension building up, I kept saying to myself, 'If he hits me I'm going to hit him back, if he hits me I'm going to hit him back.' Then his hand flew up suddenly and he smacked me on the side of the head. I didn't wait. I raised my fist and I punched him in the nose. I was ready to jump out of the car, but he didn't try to hit me again. He just drove fast, back to the apartment, where you and I got out of the car. I knew our relationship was over, so I packed my things and yours and moved out of the apartment within an hour.

"You didn't sleep well after that. You'd wake up at odd hours and tell me you were scared, but you didn't know why. Then you'd climb into bed with me and go back to sleep."

"I don't remember it," Paul said. He had unfolded his arms and looked very serious.

"I know," I said. "But I think that day upset you in ways that have never been clear to any of us. And . . . I just want you to know I'm sorry you had to go through that."

"It doesn't matter," Paul said. "He probably wouldn't have liked me anyhow."

15

The Parkers' house was an airy place. As I spent the late afternoon hours in the spacious living room with Mrs. Parker, an early spring breeze tickled wind chimes in the back hallway, which led out to an expansive backyard. Before arriving, I had imagined the house would be some sort of hovel, strewn with newspapers and used paper plates. But, in fact, the house was neat and well ordered. Mrs. Parker had greeted me at the door still wearing the same pink housedress.

I had already called her son's teachers at the private school he attended. I had formed some impressions of Peter, but before I shared them with his mother I wanted to hear what she had to say. We sat across from each other on white wicker chairs, and Mrs. Parker handed me recent photos of Peter. He was a good-looking boy, light-haired and bright-eyed. But his smile seemed forced and he didn't look at all happy to be dressed up, as he was in every picture. The clothes he wore didn't look like the clothes kids wear today. They were out of style and, if the photos weren't so glossy, I would have thought they were taken years earlier.

"I'd like to see his closet," I said when she was done showing the photos and had placed them neatly back in the big brown album that sat on her lap.

"His closet?"

"Yes," I replied.

"I can't imagine what for."

"Please," I said, "it will be helpful to me."

Mrs. Parker took me upstairs to Peter's bedroom. It was, I noticed, the biggest of the three bedrooms. There were no rock-and-roll posters on the walls. Everything was orderly. On his dresser there were plastic models of antique airplanes. A dozen outdated record albums stood in an old metal record rack. There was also a collection of Eisenhower silver dollars lined up neatly on the stand near his bed.

"There's one missing," his mother said, as I looked at the coins.

"It's his lucky dollar," Mrs. Parker said.

"What is?"

"The one that's missing."

"Good," I said, realizing that this was more evidence that Peter may have had a positive outlook when he left.

In all of Peter's wardrobe I couldn't find anything ragged. His closet was full of corduroy pants, long-sleeved shirts with button-down collars, thin neckties, and blazers. With two boys of my own at home, I knew that these were the kind of clothes most kids wouldn't want to be caught dead in.

I wasn't looking in Peter's room because of any special feeling about Peter. I had found that the room of a missing person can reveal a lot. The books on the shelf, the clothes in the closet, the notes scribbled on a pad of paper can all be hints as to why a person would disappear and where he might go.

"Did Peter pick out his own clothes?" I asked, reaching into the closet, touching the clothes.

"No," his mother said. "I buy all his clothes."

"Doesn't he have anything that's just... fun?"

"You mean modern?" she asked. "The strange things the kids wear today?"

"Yes."

"No," she said. "Just the ones he was wearing that day."

"The day he left?"

"Yes. He had on some new clothes, you know, these

crazy, colorful things that the kids are wearing. He said one of the boys at school gave them to him."

"Did you believe him?"

"I did then. Now I guess maybe he bought them with the money he took. I should have known. The clothes looked brand new."

"Where are the clothes Peter was wearing that day, before he put on the new ones?"

"Well, that's the odd thing," she said. "They seem to be gone."

We went back downstairs and talked some more about Peter, a model boy who just took off one day.

"Grades in school?" I asked.

"Peter is a straight-*A* student," she said. She sat up and smiled proudly when she said it, but it wasn't what I wanted to hear.

"Friends?"

"Oh, yes, Peter has lots of friends at school."

"How many times a week does someone come over here to visit him?"

"Oh," she said. "Well, no one's ever been here."

"Does he get phone calls from friends?" I asked.

"Well," she said, as if she had never before thought about it, "nobody has ever called for Peter."

"Then how do you know he has so many friends?" I asked.

She looked at me as if the answer were obvious. "Peter tells me about them," she said.

I asked about Peter's schedule, and again Mrs. Parker was precise to the minute when she told me what time she got Peter out of bed every morning, what time she served him breakfast, what time he left the house to catch the school bus.

"What about television?" I asked. "Does Peter have any favorite shows?"

"He watches two programs a week," she said. "Two is

all that he is allowed to watch; there's no time with school in session."

More and more I could see the profile of a youngster whose every moment was doled out and watched over by a seriously disturbed woman. Peter was a young man who had to break out of his prison.

"Mrs. Parker," I said, "you sent Peter out to catch the school bus every morning?"

"Yes, at 7:20," she said.

"Are you aware that Peter has not taken the bus to school in the last year? He's been walking two miles to school every day."

I had learned this from his teachers, and I expected his mother to be shocked.

"Is that true?" she asked.

"Yes."

She thought about it for a moment and then she smiled, again that proud smile.

"Well, there, you see," she said. "Peter's on the tennis team. He's so conscientious. He was probably running to school to keep in good shape for tennis."

I thought to myself, no, I don't think so. I believe he couldn't handle the social activity on the bus. He didn't feel good about himself. The other kids probably made fun of him because of his clothes, so he walked to school.

Mrs. Parker pulled nervously at her long hair. I could see that in the past she had been a very attractive woman. She had to know how dirty she was, I thought.

Her eyes left me for a moment, as if scanning a memory, and then she brightened a bit and smiled at me. "Would you like a cup of tea?" she asked.

"Sure," I said, feeling very sympathetic toward her at that moment.

As we walked to the kitchen I told Mrs. Parker that I wanted to search the woods behind the house while it was still light outside.

"The woods?" she asked, alarmed. "You don't think? . . ."

"No," I said, "we know that he went to Florida. I would just like to look around."

Usually, when I would poke around in backyards I wouldn't know what I was looking for and I wouldn't expect wooded areas always to yield something. When there are woods near a house, that is where children often take their secret selves, and sometimes they leave a part of those selves behind. This time I knew what I was looking for.

I found it quickly.

About thirty feet into the woods, hidden by a cluster of oak trees, there was a circle of stones where Peter had made small comforting campfires and read his magazines. Next to it was a faded pile of clothes. There was a pair of corduroy pants, a pale blue shirt, and an argyle vest. These were the clothes Peter had worn to school on the day he ran away. They were still damp from a recent rain. I lifted the pile, but as pieces of fabric began to fall from my hands, I saw that Peter hadn't just taken the clothes off, he had torn them apart. I gathered the fallen pieces together and carried them back to the house. When I walked back into the kitchen, three cups of mint tea were steeping on the counter. Don Parker had come home while I was in the woods. He greeted me with a hopeful smile, as if my presence were a signal that Peter had been found.

I showed the Parkers the torn clothes. Mr. Parker seemed to understand immediately what had happened, but Mrs. Parker just stared at them as if they were a riddle.

"Who would have done a thing like that?" she asked.

"Peter," I said softly.

"No," she said. "Never."

Mr. Parker looked at Eulla as though deep in thought. I felt it best not to speak.

The three of us went into the living room with our tea and sat down. It was time to tell them what was on my mind: "I don't know the dynamics of this family, but I know a few things about runaways. When a kid runs away, it's a symptom of an underlying problem, some anger, some anxiety perhaps. And just bringing the teenager back without dealing with the underlying problem is not good. It can even make things much worse."

"Worse?" Peter's father asked.

"Yes. Peter is obviously under a lot of pressure." I tilted my head toward the kitchen where the torn clothes were piled on a stool. "You need to consider very carefully whether you want to bring Peter back into a situation that he may not be able to handle."

"Are you saying that Peter is suicidal?" Mr. Parker asked.

"Suicide is always a possibility when a person feels he has no other way out," I told them.

"You're saying we shouldn't look for our son?" Mrs. Parker asked.

"No. I'm saying that as a family you may wish to consider counseling. Not just when Peter is back, but now, before he comes back, while we are searching for him. You are under a lot of stress that can be destructive to yourselves and your family if it is left to build up. Also, as a family, you may wish to explore why Peter may have left and how things will be when he comes back."

"I see," Mr. Parker said.

Later, after I had gathered as much information as I could from the Parkers, including the phone number of their grown daughter, Martha, Mr. Parker held my arm as he walked me to my car. I could feel that there was something on his mind.

Finally, standing out on the edge of the lawn, he looked me in the eyes. "My wife hasn't left the house by herself in nine years," he said. "She's got, what is it?"

"Agoraphobia."

"Yes, agoraphobia," he agreed. "Why do I always forget that word? Anyhow, nine years ago Eulla took the kids to Emerson Beach. The beach is on a pond not far from here. There's a beach house there, with a refreshment stand. Eulla left the kids by the water and went to get some snacks. Then she heard the screams. Both kids had gone in the water and they were in over their heads. Neither of my kids can swim. A man was swimming out to Martha. We never did find out who he was, but he saved her life. Eulla went in to get Peter, but when she got him to shore he wasn't breathing. He was cold and unconscious. Eulla got hysterical and could only stand there screaming. A bystander began mouth-to-mouth resuscitation, and someone else called an ambulance, and, thank god, they were able to revive Peter. But Eulla was never the same after that day. She blames herself."

"And she's been housebound ever since?"

"Yes," he said, "and everything has revolved around the kids, our whole social life all these years. She's got a thing about knowing where the kids are at all times. For a while we had friends whose children played with our children. We don't even have them anymore. Martha went off to college this year."

"I guess that put a lot of pressure on Peter," I said, "being his mother's whole life."

Parker sighed. "I'm sure," he said.

As I got into my car I saw a look on Mr. Parker's face that revealed a man desperate for answers which no one could give him. I wished that I could be of more help than just searching for Peter. But some things a family just has to do for itself.

I had already asked the local police department to put Peter Parker on the National Crime Information Computer (NCIC), which is maintained by the FBI. There are several million names on it, broken down into categories such as runaways, wanted persons, stolen vehicles, and so forth. Local police departments have their own computers, which can call up information from the NCIC. If, for example, Peter were picked up for vagrancy in Miami, the Miami police would run his name through the NCIC and find that he was missing. They would call the local police, who would call Peter's parents.

I called Martha, Peter's older sister. She was a student in New York City. Her parents wanted me to talk to her so that no stone would go unturned in our search for Peter.

She came to the house later that week. She was an attractive young lady, well spoken, bright. Ed was working in the office and the boys were playing upstairs, so I led her into the backyard. It was one of those balmy afternoons that will now and then make an appearance during a March cold spell, so we sat in lawn chairs by the screen door.

After our initial introduction and several minutes of small talk, Martha asked whether I thought Peter could be found.

"Of course he can be found," I said. "A runaway is pretty predictable, and the disappearances rarely become extended ones."

"But Peter is different," she said. "I think he will feel that he has committed the ultimate sin, and he will feel that he can never come home again."

From inside the house I could hear Paul's and Joey's voices rising as they were getting into an argument.

"Why do you think he ran away?" I asked.

"I don't know. Things were going fine for him, I thought, but I really can't say, because I've been away at school. I'm just not home to see things going on anymore."

Now behind me I could hear Ed in the office raising his voice to the kids upstairs, who had begun to fight again.

"Is there anything in the house that Peter might run away from or that might be bothering him?" I asked.

"No, not that I can think of," Martha replied.

"Everything with your father is okay?"

"Yes."

"Everything with your mother is okay?"

"Yes."

"There are no problems that might be of concern to Peter?"

"No, not that I am aware of," Martha said.

I found it difficult to believe that Martha would drive so far to talk to me and then have so little to say.

"*Damn it!*" I heard Ed shout. "Will you kids pipe down. I'm trying to work down here."

Through the open sliding-glass door on the patio I heard Paul yell, "Tough," and then I heard Ed's heavy footsteps as he flew up the stairs from the office.

"Would you excuse me, please," I said to Martha. I went back inside the house feeling both embarrassed and angry as I went upstairs to see what was going on.

Ed was standing in the middle of the living room, fuming and looking twice as big as he actually is. Joey was sitting in a chair and Paul was on the couch. Ed held up Paul's .22 rifle in one hand for me to see.

"Your son was handling this carelessly when I got up here," Ed said.

"Paul!" I said. "You know better than that."

Paul made a face.

"Damn it, Paul," Ed said, "don't you have any sense at all? You handle a gun with care and caution."

"It's not loaded," Paul shouted.

"You have to assume that a gun is always loaded," Ed said. "And until you understand that, you're not going to have it back."

"It's not yours," Paul yelled. "It's mine. Give it back to me."

"No," Ed said firmly.

Paul looked at the both of us.

"Well, then keep it," he shouted, getting up off the couch. Paul stomped downstairs to the front door. "Keep it. I don't live here anymore." He went out the door, slamming it behind him.

For a moment we all stood quietly.

Poor Ed, I thought. He's trying so hard with Paul, and nothing seems to work out right.

"I don't know what to do anymore," Ed said.

I knew Paul would be back in an hour. "Being irresponsible with a rifle isn't something that you can let go," I said to Ed. "Sometimes things are serious enough that you have to take a hard line. This is certainly one of those times."

I could see the look of disappointment on Ed's face. I consoled him with the few moments that I had, then reminded everyone I still had someone sitting outside on the patio.

When I got back to Martha, I apologized for the disturbance and I asked her again what there might be in her own family that would drive Peter away.

Martha thought for a moment, as if it were difficult for her to come up with something. Then she said, "Well, you know, my father has a problem with drinking and quite a temper. One time he was even fired over it."

For fifteen minutes Martha went on telling me about the things that her father had said and done while drinking. As I sat out there in the yard with Martha, trying to push the problem with Paul from my mind, I was fascinated by the fact that she had not even mentioned her mother. Not a word had been spoken. Martha talked only about her father and his drinking.

When she was done, she looked at me and waved her hands through the air as if to say, this is all I have, make what you can of it.

"Martha," I said, "what about your mother?"

"What about her?"

"Could your mother in some way have negatively affected Peter?" I asked.

"My mother is a very intelligent woman," Martha said. "Sometimes she's a little possessive about Peter, but I don't think that's a problem. She loves children, that's all."

Martha didn't mention anything about her mother fearing to leave the house for years, or anything about her personal hygiene. It wasn't my role to be a therapist, even in the most superficial sense. Yet, I felt an ethical responsibility to try to understand what it was that someone would be running from.

I discussed the case with Ed that evening, including the concern about ethical responsibility.

"You might be right," Ed said, "but that's not your decision. Your job is to find people."

We had supper that night without Paul. By ten o'clock he still hadn't come home.

16

I called Paul's friends. None of them knew where he was. I called the police and had Paul's name put on the NCI computer. I told myself that Paul would be all right, that this was probably for the best. He needed to get out into the world for a little while. It would help him mature. He would come home when he was ready. I was very reasonable, very mature about the whole thing. It was okay.

Still, I stayed up all night worrying about him and searching for an answer.

I sat on the couch in the living room, taking comfort in the spot where he had spent so much time watching television, and the questions haunted me. What did Paul need? A firmer hand? A softer touch? Did it make any difference at all? Or could a single traumatic event send a life spinning in a new direction? After all, I had seen my first husband transformed by combat. What, I wondered, is combat for a child?

The files in my office were full of runaways. Most had been found okay, or they had returned on their own. Some remained question marks. But now I really understood how all those parents had felt while they waited to see how their crisis would end.

By one o'clock in the morning I was exhausted, but I couldn't go to bed. I was worried. Three people had been murdered in our area in the past six weeks. All of them had been hitchhiking. I couldn't get it out of my mind that I was somehow responsible for my son's disappearance. Could Paul's anguish be traced to my own career?

Had I spent too much time looking for other people's kids and not enough looking after my own?

At nine in the morning my phone rang. It was a woman from Rotterdam, whom I'd met one day when I'd taken Paul to a golf course.

"Someone told me you were looking for your son," she said.

"Yes," I said.

"Well, I saw him yesterday, hitchhiking."

"Where?" I asked.

"Route 90."

"Which direction?"

"East," she said.

"It figures," I said.

Even as the mother, I couldn't shut off the detective. I had guessed all along that he would go east, try to get to I-95 and hitchhike all the way to Florida. It made sense. Paul hated cold weather. Many runaway kids on the East Coast go to Florida. We had gone to Tampa on a vacation years before and Paul had loved it. I remembered his saying, "In New York, there's a lot of time and not much to do. In Florida, there's not enough time to do all the things you want to do."

There was nothing I could do. Paul was on the NCI computer. I had spoken to all his friends. I had one hunch and a sighting, and that was all. In many of my cases there came a point at which there simply was nothing more to be done until new information came in. Now I knew firsthand the frustration those parents had known when I'd told them there was nothing more to do but wait.

I thought of going to Florida. But I didn't know for sure that he was there; and even if I did know, I wouldn't know where to begin looking. If I ran off to Florida with no plan in mind, I'd be doing exactly what I told other parents not to do.

Florida figured a lot in my thinking during this time. Peter Parker was already in Florida. Eulla Parker had called to tell me that he had been picked up in Tampa but then released again. She was angry. "They found him sleeping on a bench in the park," Eulla said. "He gave them a story about being locked out of his aunt's condo, and they believed it and let him go."

"I see," I said. "They must have let him go and then checked their computer."

"You have to go down there and find him," Eulla said.

I was tempted. It would be an excuse to look for Paul, but I knew it didn't make sense.

"It's not that simple," I told her. "We don't know where Peter is. He might even have gotten frightened by being picked up by the police. He could have left Tampa or even the state."

"Do you think he's coming home?" she asked.

"Maybe," I said. "We'll see."

A few days later I got another case that pointed to Florida.

The client's name was Harriet Montgomery. She was seventy-three years old and she wanted me to find her daughter, Jonellen.

She told me that Jonellen had been born in 1946 when Harriet and her husband were heavily involved in union politics, which sometimes got violent. When Jonellen was two years old, Mr. Montgomery had a nervous breakdown and was hospitalized. With her husband away from home, and with the labor violence increasing, Harriet became concerned that her daughter's life was in danger. She placed Jonellen with foster parents, the Cooks.

"Years went by," Mrs. Montgomery told me over the phone. Her voice sounded tired. "Years and years. I never seemed to put together enough money or the right living arrangements to bring my little girl back home to live with me."

"Did you visit her?"

"At first," she said. "But after a few years, the Cooks discouraged the visits. They said I was confusing Jonellen."

"Did you ever try to get your daughter back?"

"Yes, oh yes, we did. When Jonellen was twelve, my husband came home for good. He was well again and we wanted our little girl back. But Mr. and Mrs. Cook wouldn't let us have her. They threatened to take legal action to keep Jonellen. They said she'd be an adult in six years and she should stay with the parents she had known all those years. Maybe they were right, I don't know."

"Did you go to court?"

"No. We couldn't put Jonellen through that trauma. After that, the Cooks made it harder for us to see Jonellen. Then they moved away and they didn't tell us. All I could find out was that they had moved to Fort Myers, Florida."

"When was the last time you saw your daughter?"

"It's been twenty-two years," she said.

Twenty-two years, I thought. My son had been missing for five days and I could hardly stand it.

"Is there something compelling you to locate your daughter at this time?" I asked, half knowing the answer.

"Yes, I'm dying," she said.

Mrs. Montgomery didn't want me to bring her daughter to her. She just wanted to find the smiling little girl who by now was a forty-year-old woman.

"I just want someone to leave my house to. I want to know that Jonellen is happy and that she's all right. I want to know what she looks like. Maybe I could see a photo of her. Can you do that for me?" she asked.

I said yes, even though I knew I couldn't even guarantee that much for myself.

I talked to Paul's father almost every night. He was as worried as I was, and he promised me that things would be better when Paul came back.

I talked to Eulla Parker. Like many of my clients with missing children, she called every day. She wanted to know if there was any news.

Something wanted me to go to Florida.

17

"Something wants you to go to Florida? That's very logical," Ed said with a smile. "This is my cool, rational, analytical Marilyn talking?"

"Well, yes," I said. "Actually, I am being practical. Peter Parker is probably in Tampa. Jonellen Montgomery might still be in Florida. Paul's in Florida."

"Hold it, Marilyn, time out," Ed said. "Paul's in Florida?"

"He probably is," I said.

"What about Vermont?" Ed asked.

"Not Paul. He hates cold weather."

"What cold weather? Spring is coming."

"It doesn't matter. He's in Florida."

"I see," Ed said. "So when are you going?"

"Not me."

"No?"

He looked at me suspiciously.

"Us," I said.

"Us? As in you and me?"

"Us, as in you, me, and Joey. We're all Paul's family. It's important for him to understand that. So we should all be there to find him."

Ed stared at his newspaper for a moment. "Okay," he said. "I want to do what's best for Paul."

I took Joey out of school for a few days, and the three of us flew to Tampa.

It was late at night when we checked into a small motel.

I called the police in New York to see if there was any news on Paul.

"Sorry, ma'am. Nothing."

I left my phone number in Florida for their file. Then I dialed Eulla Parker's number to tell her where I was and to see if there was any news on Peter. An unfamiliar female voice answered the phone.

"The Parkers are not here," she said. "I'm watching the house for them. Is this Marilyn Greene?"

"Yes."

"Oh, good. Eulla's been expecting your call. Give me your number and I'll pass it on to them."

It seemed odd to me that the Parkers would go away while their son was still missing.

"Where are Mr. and Mrs. Parker?" I asked.

"Oh, I thought you knew. They're in Tampa. They flew down to help you look for Peter."

I began the next morning at the Lighthouse Mission. Still carrying my morning coffee in a Styrofoam cup, I dropped in on the two-hundred-bed shelter for the homeless and showed pictures of Peter to Father Glenn, the priest who ran the shelter on donations. Every city has too many people who can't afford to pay rent, but Tampa, with its warm weather, attracts more than most. Father Glenn was a stocky, florid-faced man who studied my pictures long and hard.

Finally he shook his head.

"I don't think so," he said. "We get them that young. Younger even. But this young man does not look familiar. Sorry."

The Lighthouse Mission was only the first of several shelters I had written on a list. It seemed to me that Peter would be afraid to sleep in the park again after getting picked up by the police and might well end up at one of the shelters. So I went to the Salvation Army and several other overnight homes, where I showed my photos of Peter to shelter workers and the drifters who gathered on the sidewalks in front of the shelters. Nobody recognized Peter.

Ed spent the day doing legwork, too. He took Peter's picture to every shelter and police station he could find.

That afternoon, Ed and Joey and I met for an early supper, then we went downtown to Bayfront Park, where Peter had been picked up by the police.

Even though Peter probably wouldn't sleep in the park again, I knew there was a chance that he would be near there. Drifters and runaways need a sense of home as much as anybody; and when they can't afford a room, they often adopt a public park, even a specific park bench, as the place they can come back to.

We spent an hour in the park, showing Peter's picture to people who were there. Nobody recognized him. Foolishly, hopefully, I pulled out a snapshot of Paul, too. "How about this boy? Have you seen him?" I asked. It seemed that my roles as mother and as investigator had merged. "No," they said.

I was feeling pretty depressed by the time I met with Don and Eulla Parker that night in their hotel room. Mrs. Parker, still wearing the pink housedress, was as worried as ever. So was Mr. Parker.

When I came in, they handed me a neatly printed list of the places where they had been looking for Peter.

"I have to tell you that I'm happy you're both here," I told them.

We stood stiffly in their deluxe bedroom. All of us were under unbearable pressure.

"We had to do something," said Mr. Parker. "Waiting had grown impossible."

"I know," I said.

They had been in Florida for days and had developed a logical plan. They had gone to music stores, video arcades, the public beaches, and other places teenagers like to go. It had occurred to them that Peter probably wouldn't have the money to buy music tapes or the change for a video game, but they felt he would seek the friendship of others his own age.

I had often cautioned parents against this kind of direct involvement, because distraught parents can make irrational decisions under stress. But this time I knew it was right. The Parkers' concern and energy could be an advantage in this case.

"I've got good news. I talked to Ken Eiland. He's a newspaper reporter I have worked with in the past on the missing-children issue. He would like to interview you and print Peter's picture."

I had expected a smile of relief from Eulla. Instead, she just stared at me as if I had delivered some tragic news.

"Oh, Marilyn, I couldn't do that," she said.

"What?" I didn't understand.

"I can't have Peter's picture printed in the newspaper."

"Why not?" I asked.

"Well, people would know he ran away."

"Mrs. Parker," I said, "thousands of kids run away. People understand."

"No," she said. "There have to be other ways."

Mr. Parker put an arm around Eulla's shoulders. He said nothing.

"Peter may still be in this area," I said. "If we run a newspaper story and photo, I think we'll have a good chance of finding him quickly. Publicity is one of the best methods of finding a missing person, if it's used correctly, and if you're sure you're looking in the right city."

"No," she said. "It's out of the question. I couldn't do it. People will think I'm not a good mother."

The Parkers exchanged a questioning look.

"No," Mr. Parker said. I had never heard him raise his voice, and now it sounded as if a new person had entered the room. "No," he said again. He placed his hands on his wife's shoulders again. "Eulla," he said, looking into her eyes, "Mrs. Greene is right. Finding Peter is the most important thing, not what people will think. Some parents would give anything for a newspaper article and photo published in the right city."

It was the first time I had heard him speak firmly to her. He looked at me. "We'll speak to the reporter," he said.

After some more conversation I left, knowing that I had done all I could do and feeling inside that the publicity would bring an end to their ordeal. They both shook my hand, and I wished them luck. "I'll phone you daily to see how things are progressing," I said as I went out the door.

By the time the newspaper story on Peter Parker was published, Ed, Joey, and I had driven to Fort Myers, where I hoped to find Jonellen Montgomery. Or Jonellen Cook. I didn't know which name she had used. To make things worse, by this time she might have had a married name.

We checked into another motel. I went through my regular routine of calling the police back home to see if any word had come on Paul.

There was nothing to report.

In the morning we got to work on the Jonellen case. Jonellen had lived in Fort Myers as a child, and if she had stayed there, I knew that a lot of public information about her would have accumulated at the county courthouse, city hall, and the offices of various state agencies. There wouldn't be any birth record, of course, but if she had gotten arrested, bought a house, or married someone, there would be a record of it.

I drove to the county courthouse, where I first checked the death records under Cook. Jonellen's foster parents would be close to eighty by now, and there was a chance that one of them had died.

I found that Mr. and Mrs. Cook had died within three days of each other in 1972. The death records gave an address, but I knew that ownership of their house would have changed. To Jonellen, I hoped.

In the real-property records, I found that the house had been owned by Jonellen Cook for three years after the Cooks had died, but the house had been sold twice since then.

As I spent the morning going through the thick gray volumes of records, I wondered if there was another private detective somewhere, who had Jonellen for a client, trying to track down Harriet Montgomery. Did Jonellen wonder about her mother? Did she ever try to find her?

It was slow, tedious work. By noon I had made some progress. I knew that Jonellen had stayed in Fort Myers into adulthood. I had been able to trace her addresses up to 1980. After that, nothing. If she had gotten married, she hadn't done it in Fort Myers.

We didn't know why Jonellen's foster parents had chosen Fort Myers for their move, but there was always the possibility that they had come to be near relatives, or that they had other children who still lived in the area. I knew that calling all the Cooks in the phone book would be a long shot, but there was a chance that one might be a relative.

Ed had spent his morning checking names in the phone book.

"What about Cooks and Montgomerys? Did you find any of interest?"

"A few," Ed said, "Jewel and Jeannine. No Jonellen. I figure either she left the area or she got married."

"You're probably right," I said, "but I don't want to miss anything."

"There's one thing," Ed said. "But it's a long shot."

"What's that?"

"One woman I talked to said there was another Cook in her class when she went to beauty school, and it was a weird first name that could have been Jonellen."

"What year?"

"Nineteen sixty-six."

"Jonellen would have been twenty," I said. "I'll check it out."

Before I returned to the courthouse for further research, I went to eat at a lunch counter. My mind was supposed to be on Jonellen, but I couldn't stop thinking about my son. While I sat waiting to be served, I flipped over the disposable place mat and I started writing down all the places I could think of that Paul had visited on our Tampa vacation. Typically, runaways go to some place familiar. I wrote down the name of the motel where we had stayed, the restaurants that I could remember, the attractions. Maybe he had gone back to one of those places looking for a job. I knew that we would go back to Tampa and I would go to every one of them. I would find my son.

Back at the courthouse after lunch, I went through the occupational-license records. If Jonellen had finished beauty school and gotten a beautician's license in the county, it would show up in the records. After an hour of searching I came upon a Jonellen Cook who had gotten a beautician's license in 1967. By 1980 she was Jonellen Davis and she opened her own beauty salon, Jonellen's.

I went to the *Yellow Pages* to see if the beauty shop was still at the same address. There it was, in a two-inch ad, "Jonellen's—we bring out the beauty in you." I've found her, I thought.

I decided to call on Jonellen in person under a pretext. I wondered how she would feel about her mother after all these years.

It was five o'clock when I got to Jonellen's Beauty Salon. It was a small, busy shop tucked into the corner of a shopping mall. At the front of the salon, a tall, fortyish woman sat behind a small table. Is this Jonellen, I wondered.

She glanced at me. "Do you have an appointment?"

"No," I said.

"We're short a girl, and we might not be able to fit you in."

She sounded as if she had come from New York. My guess was that she'd been in Florida for only a few months, however, not for twenty-five years.

"I'm here to see Jonellen. Is she here?"

"Jonellen?"

"The owner," I said.

"Oh. There isn't a Jonellen. That's just the name of the place. The owner's name is Gail."

"Are you sure?"

"Pretty sure, but I've only been working here six months, so I could be wrong. Hey, Judy, there isn't a Jonellen, is there?"

Judy was cutting somebody's hair at the back of the salon. "There used to be," she said. "She sold the place to Gail about four years ago. Gail just kept the name, that's all."

"Do you know where she went?" I called.

"Heard she opened another shop. Only it's not called Jonellen's on account of this one's called Jonellen's."

"Do you know what it is called?"

"No. Afraid I don't."

When I got back to the motel room, Ed was exhausted from making phone calls.

"No luck," Ed said, "and I'm starving. What about you?"

"Honey, do you remember that legwork I mentioned?"

"Yes."

"Well, let's have a good dinner tonight, because tomorrow we have a lot of walking to do."

The three of us spent the next morning driving from beauty salon to beauty salon to beauty salon. The county courthouse had shown no record of Jonellen opening another shop, but I knew she could be working in one. The twelfth salon we came to was across the street from a

Burger King, and we decided to stop for lunch first. It was Joey's idea.

It was a little before noon, so the restaurant was quiet. Ed and Joey sat at a table by the door while I went to the counter. After I ordered, I asked the girl behind the counter if she knew any of the people who worked at the beauty salon across the street.

"Sure," she said, "the girls come in here all the time."

"I don't suppose one of them is named Jonellen."

"Jonellen Davis? Sure, she's right over there."

"Where?"

"Right there. At that table."

She pointed to a woman in a green blouse who sat with her back to me, reading *USA Today*.

That's Jonellen! I thought to myself. I quickly turned my back to her so she couldn't see me if she happened to turn around.

"Thank you," I said to the counterwoman.

Well, Marilyn, I thought, you did it.

When I got back to the table I spoke very softly. I handed Joey his lunch. "Joey, don't say a word. Just get up and go outside quietly and get in the car."

Joey had been out on cases with me before, so he knew enough not to ask questions. He left.

"Ed, you see that lady in the green blouse?"

Ed nodded affirmatively.

"That is Jonellen Davis," I said. "Talk to her and find out whatever you can. Think of a pretext. I'm going outside so she won't see me, just in case we need a second shot at it."

I walked out of the restaurant and back to the car, where Joey and I ate our hamburgers. We also ate Ed's.

Joey and I waited in the car for what seemed like half an hour. I began to get concerned. Why was Ed taking so long?

When Ed came outside, he looked drained. "It was

hard explaining to her why I wanted to know where her shop was. I told her I had to drive my wife there for an appointment next week, and the last time we couldn't find it. She pointed out the shop by saying, 'See the front door, right in front of my Buick?' Now we have a plate number. I have a feeling this is going to be a very thorough report."

We took several photos of Jonellen as she left the restaurant. Although we were quite a distance from her at the time, the photos we took were close up and clear because of the telephoto lens on the camera.

Jonellen's mother didn't want us to contact her daughter, so I knew that the photos would be everything to her. Maybe she was right, maybe too much time had passed.

In time, I would return to Florida to deliver to Jonellen a long letter that her mother had written to her. She was the sole heir to a modest estate, but more than anything, Mrs. Montgomery just wanted to say she was sorry.

"I think I can find Paul," I said to Ed. "I'm ready to go back to Tampa."

Ed gave me a look. "Marilyn, he could just as well be in forty-nine other states."

"I don't think so. Look at it logically," I said, perhaps trying to convince us both because I knew Ed could be right. "When a teenager with a profile like Paul's runs away with no money, he'll usually go to New York City, the state of Florida, or California. Paul left at the end of March, when it was still very cold outside. I think that alone rules out New York City."

Ed wagged a finger at me. "Never rule out anything."

"Well, you know how much Paul hates the cold," I said. "The refrigerator is the only cold place he goes to voluntarily."

"True," Ed said, "very true."

"So we've got Florida and California. He's been to Florida before. He'd be more comfortable coming here because he is familiar with it. He's here, Ed, I can feel it."

"You can what?" Ed asked with raised eyebrows.

"Feel it," I repeated.

Ed laughed. "That's logical," he added. "All right, we'll go to Tampa and look for him. But first there's one extremely important step we must take before we do anything else."

"What's that?" I asked.

"We have to get some lunch. You guys ate mine."

As we pulled out of the Burger King parking lot, I was feeling both joy and sadness. I was thrilled that we had found Jonellen for her mother. But I was also sad knowing the regrets Mrs. Montgomery must have. I had a desire to help, but I knew that interfering would be the wrong thing to do.

The three of us went to a Denny's restaurant, where Ed ate lunch, then we all ate ice cream to celebrate finding Jonellen Davis.

When we got back to the motel we stumbled in, groaning to each other about the fact that we had to pack and drive all the way back to Tampa. The maid had pulled the drapes closed, and in the darkened room a red light was flashing.

"It's the message light," I said. Paul, I thought, they've found Paul. I practically jumped over the bed in my race for the phone. I picked it up and dialed the motel operator.

"You have a message to call the police in Daytona," she told me.

"Did they say what it was about?"

"No, ma'am."

I called the Daytona police. "This is Marilyn Greene," I said. They put me through to an Officer Lewis.

"Is this the Marilyn Greene from Schenectady, New York?" he asked.

"Yes," I said. My hands were shaking.

"Do you have a son, Paul Greene?"

"Yes, yes."

"Mrs. Greene, we have your son," he said.

"Oh, god. Is he all right?"

"Yes, ma'am. He seems to be pretty weak, though. We found him wandering on the beach. He said he hasn't eaten in three days."

"But he's okay?" I asked.

"Yes, he's okay. We'll keep him in custody until you get here."

Ed had come across the room to stand beside me. His arm felt comforting around me. I could feel that I was going to cry. Ed took the phone from my hand, to get directions from the officer. I sat down on the edge of the bed.

I know where my son is, I thought, but I haven't found him. Paul's running away was his way of saying he's unhappy with his life. If we just brought him back, he might run away again. It was just like the Parkers, I knew. If we didn't fix the underlying problem, we wouldn't solve anything.

Ed put the phone down. He took my hand.

"Paul says he wants to come home," he said.

18

Three months later I sat in the coffee shop of a motel in a small town in western Massachusetts. I was alone, waiting for Paul to finish packing and come have lunch with me before we drove back to Schenectady. From my table I could see through the wide picture window to the narrow black highway and the stunning view of the Berkshire Mountains beyond.

The months since Paul's return had been emotional ones for all of us. Paul and I, especially, had run the gamut. We had fought. We had cried. I told him I loved him and I was angry with him. He told me he loved me and he was angry with me. In long, sometimes torturous counseling sessions, sometimes with Ed and Joey there, all of Paul's anger came pouring out. He was angry at me; he was angry with Ed and with Chip. He was angry at God for taking away his grandmother and his grandfather. And he was angry at his father for not coming to see him.

In time, Paul and his father got to know each other. Brad came to the house, and father and son cried together, and when they had cried enough, they played together. In May, Paul had spent two weeks with his father. When he came back, he said to me, "You know, Dad really likes me. I always thought he didn't."

It was after Paul had returned from another long visit with his father that I told him about Kevin Orphman, an autistic boy who had wandered away from a school in the Berkshires three days ago. "I'm going up to search for him," I said, feeling somewhat touchy about it. The time I spent searching had been one of Paul's issues in therapy. But this time Paul surprised me.

"Can I come with you?" he asked.

"Sure," I said.

And so we spent three days searching the Massachusetts woods with Kili. People from the school had joined us, and Paul had helped them organize their part of the search.

We had not found Kevin Orphman. Now I had to go home. As I sat in the coffee shop thinking about my son and worrying about the parents of Kevin Orphman, I realized I was one of the lucky ones.

Mrs. Parker had been one of the lucky ones, too. The day after the story about Peter was published, Mr. and Mrs. Parker had gotten a call from a theater manager in Tampa. He told them that Peter was working for him, cleaning up after shows. They had taken Peter home with them and had started family therapy.

When Paul came down from the room, he was not carrying a suitcase.

"What's going on?"

"Jude Moore wants me to stay," he said. "She's going to stay and help the school manage the search. Jude thinks that I can help. They like me. Can I stay?"

"Sure," I said.

After lunch, Paul walked me to the front door of the motel. I told him I'd come back to get him in a couple of days, and I wished him luck with the search.

"When I get home can I have a dog?" he asked.

"Paul, we already have two dogs."

"I know. But I want one that's mine. You know, to train, so I can help you in searches."

"You want to go on more searches?" I asked. I could feel a tightness in my throat. Perhaps I would never find Kevin Orphman, I thought, but I had found my son.

"Sure," Paul said. "Helping to find people, what could be better than that?"

I smiled. "Nothing," I said, and I kissed him goodbye.

Light rain was falling as I crossed the parking lot. I didn't feel good about Kevin Orphman. But I knew that kids had been lost for much longer periods and still been found alive. As I drove by the entrance to the motel I saw that Paul was standing there behind the glass doors. But he wasn't looking for me. He was staring out across the highway, to the hills beyond, perhaps wondering where he would look next for the lost little boy.

Acknowledgments

The authors would like to thank Lisa Healy of Crown Publishers and our agent Evan Marshall for their enthusiasm, their support, and their hard work in helping to bring this book to life.